What others are saying about this book:

"Meier's 'Before the Nukes' is a must for those interested in the Nevada Nuclear Testing environs. Meier has provided a fascinating history of that area with many historical maps and vintage photos."

- Harold M. Agnew
former Director, Los Alamos National Lab.

"Frenchman Flat, Yucca Mountain, Pahute Mesa - names that are synonymous with the atomic history of the US - have a much earlier history that few people know. Meier has captured an important part of the opening of the West, a time when the area of the NTS was home to Indian tribes, early American pioneers, miners, and adventurers. Fascinating reading.

- Philip E. Coyle
former Associate Director, Lawrence Livermore National Lab.

"A wonderful trek through history, not only for former and current NTS workers, but for all individuals interested in the history and development of Southern and Central Nevada."

- Nick Aquilina
former Director, Department of Energy Nevada Operations Office

"'Before the Nukes' brings a new and significant contribution to the territory where our country prevailed in the Cold War. Like many of my contemporaries over four decades, I was unaware of much of the Test Site's historical past."

- Bill Flanges
former Operations Division Manager, REECo

"I thoroughly enjoyed 'Before the Nukes.' It brought back memories and insights into the history of former towns, springs, and mines that we routinely brushed against during the days of nuclear testing."

- Harold Cunningham
former President and General Manager, REECo

"Meier is passionate about his subject, and he succeeds in bringing this arid tract of land to life. 'Before the Nukes' is a must-read for all lovers of history of the American West."

Barry S. Goold
Goold Patterson Ales & Day

Before the Nukes -

Paiute Woman

Yucca Flat Today

Death Valley
Pioneers

Before the Nukes

Charles W. Meier

The remarkable history of
the area of
the Nevada Test Site

Lansinging Publications - Pleasanton, California

First printed in September 2006

10 9 8 7 6 5 4 3 2 1

Manufactured in the United States of America

Library of Congress Control Number : 2005910298
Meier, Charles W.
Before the Nukes / by Charles W. Meier
ISBN 978-0-9634749-1-9

Cover: The Mining Camp by Clyde Forsythe, Desert Publications Inc.,
        Palm Desert, CA
Collage Photos:
        Paiute Woman - Anatomy of the Nevada Test Site,
                Worman, Department of Energy
        Yucca Flat Today - Department of Energy
        Death Valley Pioneers - Death Valley in '49, The Narrative
                                                Press

Lansing Publications
P.O. Box 1887
Pleasanton, CA 94566

In memory of Frederick C. Worman, who preserved and recorded much of the history presented here.

Contents

Maps

Preface

In 1940, three million acres of the southern Nevada desert near Las Vegas were removed from the public domain and assigned to the Air Force as the Las Vegas Bombing and Gunnery Range. Ten years later, in 1950, almost one-half million acres of the Range were given to the Atomic Energy Commission to establish the Nevada Proving Grounds, later to be renamed the Nevada Test Site.

The title *Before the Nukes* was chosen to define a historical period, not to diminish the importance of the history of atomic testing, which is chronicled in many other books and documents. This is a look back to a time before there was a Nevada Test Site - a time beginning 11,000 years ago with the first occupation of the area, through a period of emigration and exploration, to a period of boom-and-bust mining. It's a history few of the tens of thousands of Test Site workers will know, as most spent busy days and nights in Mercury, the base camp, or at forward area locations in support of nuclear testing. Little time was left to roam the 1,375 square miles of remote desert and mountain terrain that are part of the Great Basin northwest of Las Vegas. Fortunately, in the early '60's, I was able to spend weekends exploring the springs, remnants of old mines, corrals, and shelters abandoned many years before by others unknown to me. Unfortunately, how much better my experiences would have been had my explorations not been made in historical ignorance. With that lesson in mind, this historical primer is meant to enrich the memories of those who have worked on the Test Site and enlighten those to come.

Acknowledgements

Doing research for *Before the Nukes* was truly rewarding as it was then I discovered how forthcoming, supportive, and helpful so many people are. The staffs at the University of Nevada Las Vegas Special Collections Library, the University of Nevada Reno Special Collections Library, and the University of Nevada Reno Mackay School of Earth Sciences and Engineering were of great assistance. Also most helpful were the staffs at the Nevada State Historical Society, Reno and the Nevada State Museum, Carson City, Nevada. A special thanks to Eva La Rue, Director, Central Nevada Museum, for her assistance in locating photos of the Las Vegas and Tonopah Railroad. The Department of Energy, National Nuclear Security Administration Nevada Site Office (*formerly DOE Nevada Operations Office*), maintains historical records for the Nevada Test Site. They have been generous in providing photos and historical narratives that were the springboard for my research. Troy Wade, President of the Nevada Test Site Historical Foundation and Bill Johnson, Director of the Atomic Testing Museum, Las Vegas, Nevada provided helpful comments and encouragement after reviewing the manuscript, which still needed work.

Finally, by serendipitous luck while researching the paintings of Clyde Forsythe, I met attorney Barry Goold of Goold Patterson Ales & Day, Las Vegas. Barry has a love of all things western and his collection includes two paintings by Forsythe. He patiently spent hours laboring over my manuscript, providing invaluable comments. His efforts have made my "engineering prose" much more readable, and we can all thank him for that.

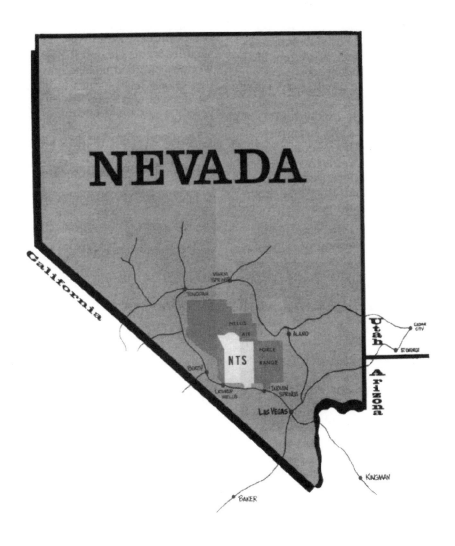

Nevada Test Site location map - Source: Department of Energy

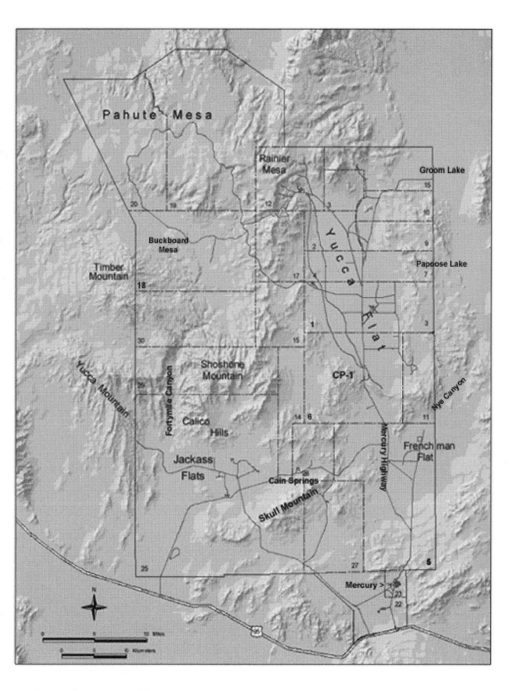

NTS relief map (modified to show salient sites) - Source: Department of Energy
Nevada Operations Office

The Setting

Papoose Dry Lake, eastern edge of Yucca Flat - Photo courtesy of Prof. James L. Reveal, University of Maryland

"We journeyed fifty miles with the Timpahute, and descended into the first real desert I had ever seen, and saw here, for the first time, the mirage. We had been without water for twenty-four hours, when suddenly there broke into view to the south a splendid sheet of water, which all of us believed was Owen's Lake. As we hurried towards it the vision faded, and near midnight we halted on the rim of a basin of mud, with a shallow pool of brine."

Those are the despondent words of Rev. John Wells Brier of the ill-fated Death Valley '49er Party describing his entry into the area of the Nevada Test Site near Papoose Dry Lake in December 1849. Today, as then, the NTS remains a foreboding, barren, and desolate area despite the recent evidences of nuclear testing - isolated buildings and dry lakes pockmarked by underground nuclear explosions. Standing in Yucca Flat, the panorama is visually open for miles - the distance closed in by majestically rugged mountains. From this vantage point there is no mistaking that, despite its beauty, this is an area hostile to human habitation. Rainfall is scarce. There are no rivers and the only lakes are dry. Seven scattered springs are nature's only offer of water in an area that is larger than the state of Rhode Island. The aridness of the area is immediately apparent from the vegetation - predominantly sage, creosote, and blackbrush, with Joshua and pinyon pine trees at higher elevations. Only twentieth century technology has made sustained living and working on the NTS palatable. Deep wells, tapping ancient aquifers, and endless power lines serve the Department of Energy's workforce that has numbered as high as 10,000 during the peak of the cold war nuclear testing days, but now hovers around 2,000.

The NTS lies in the transition zone between the Mojave Desert and the Great Basin. The site is bounded by U.S. Highway 95 on the south and rimmed on the west, north, and east by mountains and valleys that are part of the Nellis Air Force Range. Within the site are three major valleys - Yucca Flat at the north end, Frenchman Flat to the south, and Jackass Flat to the southwest. Yucca and Frenchman Flats contain large dry lake areas that were the sites of aboveground and underground nuclear tests. Jackass Flat is the former site of the Rover Project, a nuclear rocket development project, and the Pluto Project, a nuclear ramjet propulsion project. Elevations on the Site vary from 2,730 feet at Jackass Flat, at the extreme southwest corner of the site, to 7,712 feet on Pahute Mesa in the Eleana Range in the northwest corner. To the south is the Amargosa Valley, a broad, flat, arid, and treeless valley. Death Valley is a scant 50 miles from the southern edge of the NTS. The much-publicized "secret" Air Force base at Area 51 lies next to Groom Lake , just off the northeast corner of the NTS.

Springs On the NTS

Cane Springs and buildings - Source: Anatomy of the NTS, Frederick C. Worman

As with any arid location, water is the most important resource affecting the lives of the inhabitant or transient. On the NTS, springs were the only source of water and it was there that archeologists found signs of historic and prehistoric inhabitants. While seeps exist at several locations on hillsides, there are seven named springs on the NTS as shown on the nearby map: Cane Spring, Tippipah Spring, Topopah Spring, Captain Jack Spring, White Rock Spring, Oak Spring, and Tub Spring. *Often in references, the words spring and springs are used interchangeably and you will find that throughout this book.* Tippipah means "little water" and Topopah means "big water," in the Paiute language. Captain Jack Spring was named for

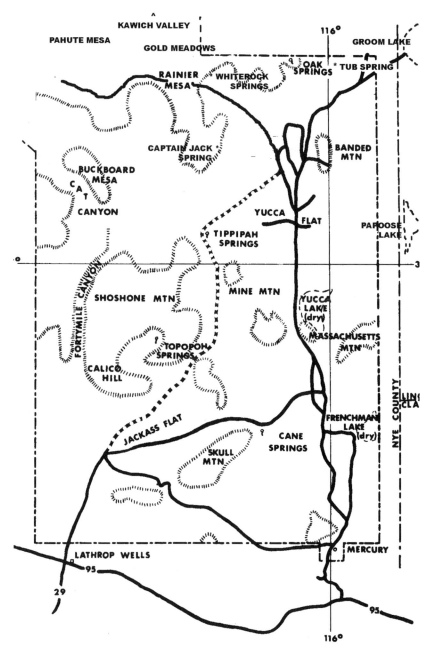

Map of the NTS (modified to show springs) - Source: Anatomy of the Nevada Test Site, Frederick C. Worman

Captain Jack who carried mail over the pack trail from Utah to the Groom Mine, just above Groom Lake. Far from being an oasis in the desert, the discharge rate of these springs is typically a gallon per minute or less. As shown in the accompanying photos, with the exception of Cane Spring, the ponding areas around these springs were quite small. For the water-desperate traveler, the chances of an adequate water supply at any spring was problematic. Nonetheless, they were often life saving for animals and humans in desperate need of water. While today, a trip between springs is made in less than an hour, in 1906, a party headed by USGS surveyor Robert Chapman traveling by horseback and wagon remarked that the trip from Oak Springs to Cane Springs had taken three days "and the distance is not more than 35 miles."

White Rock Spring - Source: Anatomy of the NTS, Frederick C. Worman

Captain Jack Spring - Source: Archeological Investigations at the U.S. AEC's Nevada Test Site and Nuclear Rocket Development Station, Frederick C. Worman

Cabin at White Rock Spring - Source: Archeological Investigations at the U. S. AEC's Nevada Test Site and Nuclear Rocket Development Station, Frederick C. Worman

Before the Nukes

The First Inhabitants

"Occupation for generations, and even hundreds of years, in such inhospitable places as the Nevada Test Site and even in Death Valley, is a tribute to man's ability to adapt to nearly any environment."
Frederick C. Worman

It is paradoxical that very little was written about the archeology of the area occupied by NTS until it became a nuclear test site. In the early twentieth century, the mining period, few were interested. Later in the century, Nevada historians became interested, but access was severely limited when the area became part of the Las Vegas Bombing Range and subsequently the Nevada Test Site. In 1969, Frederick C. Worman, Los Alamos Scientific Laboratory, produced a document titled "Archeological Investigations at the U.S. Atomic Energy Commission's Nevada Test Site and Nuclear Rocket Development Station." Subsequent efforts by archeologists at the Desert Research Institute have preserved and enhanced the research started by Worman. To their collective credit and through their efforts, much of the historic and prehistoric information about the area of the Test Site was documented and is presented here. The cultural chronology of Native American occupation of the Test Site is graphically shown at the bottom of the next few pages, *dated in years before present day.*

Occupation of the area began as far back as 10,500 BCE, the Pleistocene Big Game Hunter period. This was 2,000 years before the Bering Strait Land Mass was submerged, closing off the migration land route from Asia to North America. It is probable that early occupation was sporadic with small family bands making seasonal hunting and gathering forays. Pollen studies have indicated the presence of more rainfall during the days of the early Paleo-Indian hunters than at present. Juniper pollens have been found in Pleistocene packrat nests at locations far from the present location of those trees. Juniper trees require a 10-15 inch annual rainfall compared to less than 5 inches at present in the area of the packrat nests. Radiocarbon dates place the age of some nests at about 10,000 years ago. This was a period, about 9,000 to 7,000 years ago, called the Anathermal, a cool period that became progressively warmer. During this period, there was more moisture than at present. This relatively moist period was followed by the Altithermal, a period of high temperature and dryness which lasted from 7,000 to 4,000 years ago. The harsh conditions of the Altithermal period resulted in reduced human populations, with evidence that entire areas of the Mojave and Great Basin deserts

were abandoned. For the last 4,000 years, the Test Site has been in the Medithermal period, characterized by more moderate temperatures and increased moisture.

The earliest date of habitation in the area is inferred from the finding of Clovis materials on the Test Site and in nearby areas. A Clovis Point found in Area 30 (Buggy Site) by Don McGuffin , Lawrence Radiation Laboratory, is shown at the left. Clovis artifacts are named after the site at Clovis, New Mexico where they were first found and are associated with Paleo-Indians who settled in North America about

Clovis	San Dieguito I		San Dieguito II & III		
12,000	11,000	10,000	9,000	8,000	7,000

Before the Nukes

11,500 years ago. They were big game hunters who produced distinctive spear points, which were thin and tapered, flaked on both sides, and fluted at the base to facilitate attachment to a shaft. The fluting served another purpose as it increased the blood flow from a wounded animal, accelerating death. The Clovis people apparently came to North America over the Bering Land Mass. Clovis artifacts have been discovered in all 48 contiguous states.

At the Clovis, New Mexico site, as well as others, Clovis points were found in association with the remains of the extinct fauna, primarily the mammoth. It is assumed that climatic conditions in the area of the NTS some 12,000 years ago were compatible with the requirements of the larger mammals such as the mammoth and ground sloth, which lived at the end of the Pleistocene epoch. The Clovis culture was followed by the Folsom culture, 11,000 - 10,000 BP. Folsom were hunters of the giant bison and their fluted points have been well established as offspring of the Clovis by dating techniques and stratigraphy. While nearby sites show evidence of the Folsom, only evidence of the San Dieguito culture has been found on the Test Site.

Early Cultures

Evidence of the many cultures that traversed the Test Site and stayed for varying periods of time has been found in several locations, predominantly springs, rock shelters, caves, and even petroglyphs. From this evidence, archeologists pieced together the probable cultures of the area. Most of the evidence is in the form of pottery sherds (aka shards), projectile points, and ceramic and non-ceramic artifacts that aid in identifying and dating the various cul-

	Amargosa I	Amargosa II		Amargosa III	
6,000	5,000		4,000	3,000	2,000

Years before Present Day

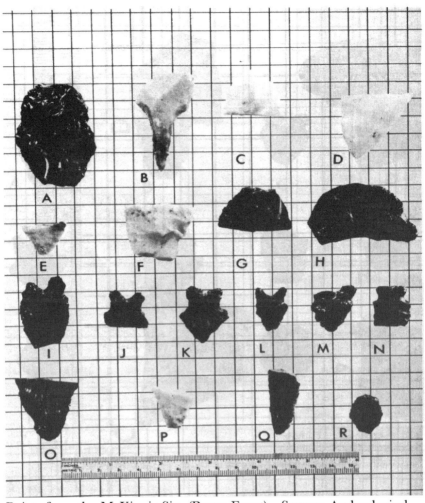

Points from the McKinnis Site (Buggy Event) - Source: Archeological Investigations of the U.S. AEC's Nevada Test Site and Nuclear Rocket Development Station, Frederick C. Worman

(A) Knife, San Dieguito III (B) Drill, chalcedony (C) Partial Knife (D) Partial Knife (E) Partial Knife, chalcedony (F) Partial Knife, white chert (G) Partial Knife, obsidian (H) Partial Knife (I) Partial Point (J) Partial point, Pinto Basin type (K) Point (L): Point, Pinto Basin type (M) Point (N) Partial Point (O) Partial Knife (P) Partial Knife (Q) Point (R) Scraper

tures. Projectile points (arrowheads, spearheads, scrapers, choppers, axes, etc.) are particularly useful for identifying cultures and dating their existence on the Test Site because there is a large database on the style, materials, and sophistication of the points used by various peoples. An example of the various projectile points found on the Test Site in shown on the preceding page. These are from the McKinnis site, named for William McKinnis of (then) Lawrence Radiation Laboratory. McKinnis notified Worman of the archeological importance of the site in Area 30 prior to its use for the Buggy event. Worman considered this one of the most interesting and important sites examined and subsequently documented and preserved many of the artifacts. The site was buried under 48 feet of overburden with detonation of Buggy, a test of the peaceful use of nuclear explosives for earth moving.

After the Pleistocene Big Game Hunters, the next culture to occupy areas of the NTS was the San Dieguito peoples, more than 11,000 years ago. The existence of the San Dieguito peoples is evidenced by Lake Mojave-style projectile points found in the Yucca Mountain area and at Cane Spring. The San Dieguito were hunters who also collected wild plants and did some fishing. During this period, there were marsh areas and pluvial lakes that formed in the valleys. No evidence indicates that the basins on the Test Site supported lakes, but nearby valleys immediately to the east and to the north apparently did.

Worman referred to the makers of the Pinto, Elko, and Gypsum projectile points as the Amargosans. The Amargosans were a culture that is believed to have moved from southern Utah, crossing southern Nevada into the Mohave Desert and other parts of California during the period 7,000 to 2,000 years ago. Amargosan-

Basketmaker	Pueblo/Anasazi	Numa (Paiute/Shoshone)
2,000	1,000	

Years before Present Day

The First Inhabitants

style projectile points have been found in several areas of the Test Site, mostly at the higher elevations. An example of an Amargosan-style point found on Rainier Mesa-Gold Meadows area (McKinnis Collection) is shown to the left.

The Basketmaker culture followed the Amargosans, but Worman had difficulty separating the Amargosans and the early Basketmakers and believes that they may have been one and the same. The early Basketmakers dwelled in makeshift houses and lived on small game and wild vegetables. The bow and arrow was unknown to them, but the atlatl, or spear thrower, was in use for hunting game.

Throwing a spear using an atlatl - Courtesy of the Ohio Historical Society

The later Basketmaker culture was a manifestation of the earlier culture, with the addition of agricultural pursuits, the bow

Before the Nukes

and arrow, and finally pottery making. All of these brought about a more sedentary existence, which eventually led to the more highly sophisticated Pueblo culture.

The finding of Anasazi (early Pueblo) pottery in the Yucca Mountain area and other locations indicates that the Pueblo peoples may have entered the area of the Test Site or at least traded their pottery to its occupants. Lino Gray, a type of Pueblo pottery found on the Test Site, has been dated to before 750 AD. The Pueblo peoples appear to have left southern Nevada about 800 years ago.

The last Indians to occupy the NTS were the Southern Paiute and Shoshone, also referred to as the Numa. Caves, such as "Big

Paiute artifacts from Fortymile Canyon - Source: Anatomy of the Nevada Test Site, Frederick C. Worman. All three bowls are of the type known as Southern Paiute utility brownware. Grinding stones shown are for grinding wild seeds.

Pahute Mesa Rockshelter #6, Area 19 - Source: Archeological Investigations at the U.S. AEC's Nevada Test Site and Nuclear Rocket Development Station, Frederick C. Worman

George's" (see also *Petroglyphs on the NTS, pg. 17*) located on the south side of Cat Canyon, and rock shelters, such as the one pictured on Pahute Mesa, contained large numbers of beads and other trade materials documenting the Paiute occupation of the NTS into historic times. Several dark blue glass beads, made in Italy and known as "Hudson's Bay Beads," were found, indicating trade with tribes to the north sometime after 1850.

Test Site historian Lonnie Pippin writes that when the first Euro-American explorers and immigrants entered southern Nevada, they encountered widely scattered groups of hunters and gatherers calling themselves Numa, Numos, Numes, and Nunas. They were well adapted to an environment that seemed harsh even to hardy early explorers. The Numa were annual migrators following the seasonal availibility of plants and animals. Semi-permanent base camps were established by groups, most often related families, where food, fuel, and water could be stored for use during the winter. Pinyon pine nuts were a major staple gathered at the higher elevations; however, maintaining a population over an extended period of time required game to supplement stored pinyon nuts. Individual game hunting was common, but relatively inefficient. Communal game drives were more efficient and generally held during the spring or fall when peoples gathered at residential bases. Yucca Flat was a location of communal rabbit drives, which lasted for as long as a month. A series of large nets, typically 3 feet high and 50 to 100 feet long, were stretched across the flat and propped up with sticks. A hunting party beat the brush while others stood behind the nets with clubs or bow and arrows. Other Western Shoshone communal activities included a social dance or *fandango*, often held in conjunction with the pine nut harvest or hunting seasons. Here participants could share information on the location and abundance of critical resources such as water, deer, and pinyon nuts.

William Manly and other Death Valley Forty-niners write of their contact with Indians in the winter of 1849 as they passed through the NTS. Their trip across the NTS is discussed in detail later. Between 1875 and 1880, at least nine Shoshone families or family groups maintained winter campsites on the NTS. By the early twentieth century, most of the free-roaming Native Americans had moved to surrounding towns or relocated to reservations. The remains of a Paiute wickiup at NTS are shown in the photograph on the next page. Today, tribes still access the NTS for the use of ceremonial resources.

Paiute wickiup or dwelling on the Test Site, probably inhabited around the turn of the 20th century - Source: Anatomy of the Nevada Test Site, Frederick C. Worman

Petroglyphs on the NTS

Native American petroglyph in Fortymile Canyon - Source: Department of Energy

Upper Fortymile Canyon and Cat Canyon are rich with Great Basin rock art, specifically petroglyphs. A total of 2,921 petroglyph elements on 482 boulders and panels have been recorded. These historic areas constitute some of the most significant and earliest recorded archeological sites on the NTS and in southern Nevada. Fortymile Canyon was an important prehistoric travel route between the low-lying areas to the south and the higher elevations to the north. The rock art in the canyon represented a significant setting, perhaps ritual, for the travelers. Western Shoshone also traveled this route in the late 1800's to harvest pinyon nuts or to participate in rabbit hunts. The time-dated artifacts of the largest site in Fortymile Canyon indicate repeated use over thousands of years. Based on the density and variation of the archeological remains, the site was a location where people stayed for periods of time as opposed to brief or overnight excursions.

At the intersection of Fortymile Canyon and Brushy Canyon

Fortymile Canyon looking south - Source: Department of Energy

is the area of Big George's Cave, one of the largest rock art sites in southern Nevada. A photograph of Big George's Cave, also known as Prospector's Cave, is shown in the chapter "Mining on the NTS." Supposedly, Jack "Big" George was a Western Shoshone living at the site in the early part of the 20th century. The George family moved horses through the canyon to Kawich Valley and stayed at the cave. While there was no rock art inside the cave, rock art is extensive over the surrounding site. Some boulders are covered on all faces, even the bottoms, with designs. According to American Indian consultants, the site was a place where different ethnic groups (such as the Southern Paiute and Western Shoshone) camped, gathered and processed food, and conducted ceremonies. Excavated artifacts from the area suggest that the site was visited throughout history beginning in the early to middle Holocene epoch, which began 10,000 years ago.

Before the Nukes

Early Exploration

Prior to the crossing of the NTS in 1849 by the ill-fated Death Valley '49ers, there is scant documentation about exploration in the area. Jedediah Smith, a fur trapper and explorer, passed through Nye County in 1827, but his route was north of Tonopah and not on the NTS. In the spring of 1844, John C. Fremont passed south of the NTS in the area of Pahrump Valley. In 1845, Fremont passed north of the NTS in the area of Tonopah and the Toiyabe Range.

In 1848, he published a map of the Great Basin. It is this map that may have played a part in the saga of the Death Valley '49ers.

Worman writes that "the first evidence of white penetration into the NTS is a stone block inscribed

F. O. BYOR rock, Univ. of Nevada Reno, W. M. Keck Earth Science and Engineering Museum

with the name "F. O. BYOR" and the date "1847." The block was picked up and likely used at a later date in the construction of the fireplace of the stone cabin at Cane Springs since, according to local construction practice, the stone house was built in the 1870's or later. The mystery of the origin of the stone is discussed by Dr. Margaret Long, in her fascinating book, "The Shadow of the Arrow." Dr. Long notes there were a number of legends regarding the stone, but believes that members of the Mormon Battalion

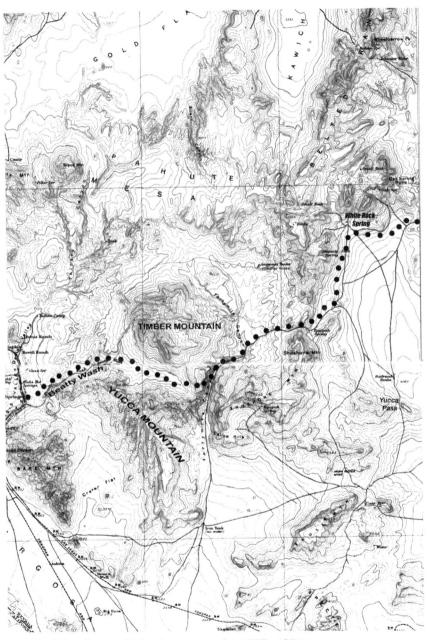

Route of Lt. George Wheeler across the NTS, 1871

Before the Nukes

wandered into this region in 1847 and that a member of the Battalion may have carved it. Dr. Long based her belief on a conversation with Governor Scrugham of Nevada, who was interested in the antiquities of the state and told her that the Battalion had a guide, a Frenchman in the area named La Quinta or Naquinta and for whom Frenchman's Flat was named. The Governor believed it likely that La Quinta would have known of Cane Springs where the block was found. *It appears the legend is unfounded.* A search of the Mormon Battalion records by Terry Wirth, Trails Officer, showed that F. O. Byor was not a member. Further, the Mormon Battalion return route was southeast of the Test Site along the Old Spanish Trail. The mystery of who F. O. Byor was and why he was at Cane Springs remains.

In 1871, a survey party sponsored by the U. S. Army and led by Lieutenant George M. Wheeler entered the area of the NTS. The expedition had about 80 men split into two parties to cover more territory. The half under Wheeler's direct command camped at White Rock Spring after a visit to the Pahranagat mines, north of the NTS. They then proceeded to Tippipah Spring and crossed the headwaters to Fortymile Canyon, south of Buckboard Mesa. From there they ventured along the slopes of Timber Mountain, north of Yucca Mountain to Beatty Wash, and onto the Amargosa River in the Oasis Valley near present day Beatty.

For the remainder of the 19th century, with the exception of a poorly documented freight and mail route between Salt Lake city and Los Angeles which may have run through Fortymile Canyon in the 1870's, there is little information on the Fortymile Canyon area.

No further activity in the area is recorded until the start of the mining boom in the Bullfrog District, two miles west of Beatty, in the summer of 1904. The town of Rhyolite grew rapidly. By 1907, it was a major metropolis of 6,000 inhabitants. The immedi-

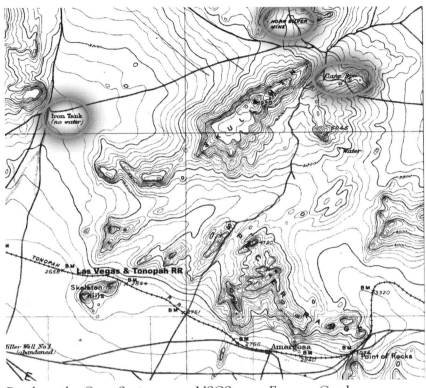

Roads in the Cane Springs area, USGS map, Furnace Creek
Quadrangle, 1910

ate effect of the new mining activity in the area was to increase
traffic between Las Vegas and the Bullfrog District with daily stages
bringing passengers, express, and mail. On June 10, 1905, the first
stage run by the Utah and Nevada Express Company left Las Vegas
for Bullfrog. This stage line used the new Miller Toll Road, which
was advertised as a shorter route than the existing road. The Miller
Toll Road ran close to the present location of State route 95. Stations on the Miller road near Yucca Mountain included Fortymile
Wash and Cane Springs. Both stations offered bars, as well as
eating and lodging facilities. The station on Fortymile Wash was
called Iron Tanks. Water was hauled there and sold. At Cane
Springs, where a 3,000-gallon tank had been built, water was avail-

Before the Nukes

able without charge. Cane Springs also served as the main layover point. B. F. Miller, the general manager of the stage line and owner of the toll road franchise, lived there with his family. The shortcut was not a success: the stage was discontinued in August 1905, due to the limited water supply. Despite efforts by Miller to improve water facilities at Cane Springs, the stage was not revived. This route ceased to be important in 1906 with the completion of the Las Vegas and Tonopah Railroad, which operated between Las Vegas and Goldfield until 1918.

In 1936, Norman Carr was lost while prospecting at Fortymile Wash near the south end of Yucca Mountain and died before he could relocate his vehicle. His body was found by Death Valley Curley (*Roscoe C. Wright - see photo, pg. 35*) who had tracked Carr's movements across the desert. In 1940, Death Valley Curley led archaeologist Sidney M. Wheeler and his companions into Fortymile country. In addition to the aboriginal sites and mineral deposits, the party visited a rock spire in the headwaters of Fortymile Canyon near Tippipah Spring. The spire was carved with the inscription "BY FOGLE 1863." Lore has it that this monument is connected to the legendary Lost Breyfogle Mine,

BY FOGLE carved rock, Fortymile Canyon - Source: Nevada Historical Society

one of the more famous lost mines of the southwest. Is this credible? *Perhaps!* Charles Breyfogle, along with his brother, Joshua, were part of the California '49ers, spending time in the mining camps east of Sacramento. In 1850, Charles Breyfogle returned to his home in upstate New York with $20,000 in gold. A year later, he would return to California where, for a time, he served as county assessor in Oakland. In 1863, Breyfogle was lured by Nevada's silver bonanzas to Tonopah. There, through a bizarre set of circumstances, he joined with three other men headed for Texas, not for gold or silver, but to join the Confederacy. Camped in an area south of Ash Meadows, he and his three comrades were attacked by hostile Indians. Breyfogle managed to escape, but his three friends were killed. He wandered the desert for several days until he found a spring (Tippipah?). While resting there, he discovered a vein of rich gold-bearing quartz and packed several samples. But the riches of a gold strike were to elude him. He was again captured and held by Indians for months before finally being ransomed to a passing wagon train of Mormons. Nursed back to health, Breyfogle headed many search parties over the next 26 years in search of the vein of gold that would make him rich, but to no avail. There are many versions of this story, some saying that the Johnnie Mine, on the north end of Pahrumph Valley, and the Lost Breyfogle Mine are one and the same; however, the legend that it remains lost still persists.

It is interesting to ponder whether or not Breyfogle would have connected his journey in the area of the Nevada Test Site with that of the famous "Jayhawker Party," just four years before him. The Jayhawkers were part of the well chronicled "Death Valley '49ers." Surely Breyfogle would have heard of them in his travels in the gold camps of northern California. The Jayhawker's path to Death Valley and infamy was across the Test Site. That story is told in the next chapter.

The Death Valley '49ers Cross the NTS

In the winter of 1849, tragedy beset a small group of pioneers bound from Salt Lake City to the gold fields of California. In a belief that they were taking a shortcut route to Los Angeles, they crossed the area of southern Nevada now bounded by the Nevada Test Site. Exiting the southern boundary of the Test Site, they would join up with others lost and desperately seeking a way over the Panamint Range of the southern Sierra Nevada Mountains. Their story is told in engrossing detail by one of the party, William Lewis Manly, in his book "Death Valley in '49." Based on accounts by Manly and others, George Koenig, in his book, "Beyond This Place There Be Dragons," painstakingly reconstructs the routes taken by the '49ers across the Test Site (*see map, page 31*). The trek of this group of pioneers, including women and children, across the Test Site would prove nearly as harrowing as the tribulations they would later face crossing the "Valley of Death."

During the fall of 1849, a steady stream of emigrant wagons from the east moved westward towards Salt Lake City along the Platte River and South Pass. Salt Lake City was the meeting point of the great pioneer trails to the Pacific coast and the cutoffs to and from them. From the east, the Mormon Trail came in from Fort Bridger, Wyoming, on the Oregon Trail. Due west, across the Great Salt Lake Desert, the Hastings Cutoff used by the Donner Party led to the California Trail on the Humboldt River in Nevada. Of particular interest this late in the year was a route to the south connecting with the Old Spanish Trail from Santa Fe, giving access to the gold fields by way of southern California. It was the longest route, but avoided the higher altitudes and early winter snows of the Sierras that had sealed the fate of the Donner Party three years earlier.

The emigrants who reached Salt Lake City in the fall of 1849 were faced with a dilemma. The Donner Party disaster provided fair warning for those who might think of crossing the northern Sierras in the early winter. Since most of the emigrants were of humble means, they had only enough necessities to carry them through on a schedule that did not include a winter layover. With little money, no available work, and a scarcity of supplies, they were desperate to continue on to California. Amidst their despondency came a Captain Jefferson Hunt who offered to guide them to San Bernardino for the sum of $10 a wagon. They had heard rumors of a southward route to California, but as Manly writes, "No wagons were reported as ever getting through that way, but a trail had been traveled through that barren desert country for perhaps a hundred years and the same could be easily broadened into a wagon road." Despite well-voiced concerns by many, in early October, Hunt's wagon train began to move south. Manly writes of "107 wagons, a big drove of horses and cattle, perhaps 500 in all."

The route they were following connected to the Old Spanish Trail from Santa Fe to Los Angeles by way of Las Vegas. During the journey south, there was news of a map showing a shortcut. Historians agree that the map was real, but are uncertain of its origin. It was variously attributed to "a Williams of Salt Lake" or "a Captain Smith," while some said it was one of Fremont's maps. On November 4, 1849, after much discussion at a camp near present day Cedar City, Utah, all but seven wagons abandoned the route to Los Angeles by way of Las Vegas and the Santa Fe Trail. They had been lured by the illusory promise of a more direct, but unexplored route that would shorten the trip to the gold fields by several hundred miles. Like the Donner party, it was a choice they would later regret. Captain Hunt said that if all decided to go (on the cutoff), "I will go with you, even if the road leads to Hell." However, he made clear his heartfelt obligation to those who wanted to continue on the original route, stating that "Even if one wagon decides to go the original route, I shall feel bound to go with that wagon." True to his promise, Captain Hunt moved south towards Las Vegas with those who wished to continue on to Los Angeles via the Santa Fe Trail.

Three days after turning off the main trail, the '49ers reached an area near Mt. Misery, straddling the Utah-Nevada border. Manly notes, "Immediately in front of us was a canyon, impassible for wagons, and down into this the trail descended. Men could go, horses and mules, perhaps, but wagons could no longer follow that trail." Scouts were sent out to search for a pass. After a few days, the enthusiasm about the Smith cutoff began to die and there was talk of going back to follow Captain Hunt. "On the third morning a lone traveler with a small wagon and one yoke of oxen died. He seemed to be on this journey to seek to regain his health. He was from Kentucky, but I have forgotten his name." Returning scouts reported there was no way to go further with the wagons. With this news, many of the wagons turned back to rejoin the party led by Captain Hunt. Finally, a party returned with the news that a pass had been found and "no trouble could be seen ahead." About 27 wagons remained when this news came and they agreed to travel on westward and not go back to the old trail. The group consisted of 63 persons, including three women and seven children, ages one to 11 years. The wagons were those of the Bennett-Arcan party of 14 persons including Sarah Bennett, Abigail Arcan, four children, and Manly and John Rodgers, who were traveling with them; Sheldon Young, who was traveling as an independent; the Reverend John Welsh Brier party of seven persons, including Juliet Brier and their three children; the Savage-Pinney party of 11 men; and the Jayhawkers, described as "thirty single men" that included Asa Haynes who, like Manly, would keep a log of their trip. Together, these pioneers would cross the NTS and suffer unimaginable privations on their way to a place etched in history.

The Jayhawker party, comprised of young men, often took the lead. The term "Jayhawker" did not refer to a Kansan in 1849. The men were, in fact, from Knox County, Illinois. It is conjectured that the name embodied the feisty characteristics of the jaybird with the swift and powerful anatomy of a hawk, capable of surviving when death seemed inescapable. According to Jayhawker John B. Colton, he guessed the group adopted the name as "it was the meanest thing they could think of."

Very little is known about the Savage-Pinney party, referred to as a group of nine or eleven, who left the main party and proceeded west packing their food on their backs. Savage and Pinney reached the gold fields near Nevada City, but the other nine disappear into history.

The Brier party consisted of Rev. John Welsh Brier (age 35), his wife Juliette (Juliet/Julia), three sons, Christopher (age eight), John (age six), and Kirke (age four). Two others in the party were variously referred to by the Briers as Lommis and Patrick or "two Germans" and may have been part of one of the other parties. Rev. Brier was a Methodist minister from Iowa City. Juliet Brier (age 35) was born in Bennington, Vermont, in 1813 and educated in a Vermont seminary. While only a slip of a woman, she would turn out to be the strongest. In his book, "Some Strange Corners of Our Country," published in 1892, Charles Lummis wrote:

> The strongest of the whole party was wee, nervous Mrs. Brier ... who shared with her boys of four, seven, and nine years that indescribable tramp of nine hundred miles. For the last three weeks

she had to lift her athletic husband from the ground every morning, and steady him for a few moments before he could stand; and help wasted giants who, a few month before, could have held her upon their palms.

West of Mt. Misery, the Savage-Pinney party separated from the train and moved south and west to eventually cross the NTS in the area of Frenchman Flat and pass through Jackass Flat. The remaining (main) party, now consisting of the Jayhawkers, Manly, Rogers, the Bennett-Arcans, Young, the Wades, the Nusbaumers, the Haynes, and the Briers moved west and north crossing an area between the Nevada cities of Caliente and Panaca on now Highway 93. Near the end of November, after more than two weeks of wandering, they finally abandoned their westward trek and turned south following the Penoyer Valley to the area of Sand Springs. "They had now covered about 300 miles from Mt. Misery and each mile was becoming longer than the one before."

At Sand Springs Dry Lake, some 30 miles north of Groom Lake and the edge of the NTS, the desolate expanse of the valley stretched out before them. There were no signs of water or grass as far as the eye could see. Oxen were beginning to fail. They searched individually and collectively for water and even the poorest of grazing. Accounts vary in detail, but one or two Indians were captured. Manly recounts an Indian who showed them "a small ravine four miles away which had water in it, enough for our use," at which point the Indian bounded away "after the fashion of a mountain sheep." It was at Sand Springs that Haynes elected to take the route through Desert Valley on the east side of the Timpahutes. The Nusbaumers joined the Bennett-Arcans and move southward toward Groom Lake and the north edge of the NTS.

The '49ers Enter the NTS

Overlooking Papoose Dry Lake in the distance, circa 1928 - Source: Shadow of the Arrow, Margaret Long, photo by Pierce Long

The next camp they made came to be referred to as "Last Camp," as it was the last camp that the parties would be together. Koenig considers all accounts of the location of Last Camp and concludes that the highest probability is that it was Papoose Dry Lake, just off the northeast edge of the NTS. The faster-moving parties, the Jayhawkers and Bennett-Arcans, arrived at the end of November while the slower moving Wades and Briers would arrive late the evening of December 1st.

John Brier, Jr., who was 7 or 8 at the time, recalled:

> "We had all been without water for twenty-four hours, when suddenly there broke into view to the south a splendid sheet of water, which all of us believed was Owen's Lake. As we hurried towards it the vision faded, and near midnight we halted on the rim of a basin of mud, with a shallow pool of brine."

Asa Haynes, a member of the Jayhawkers, reported in his log,

Before the Nukes

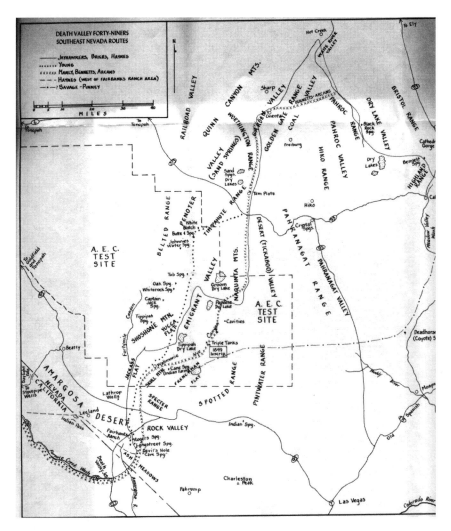

Probable routes of the Death Valley '49ers across the NTS - Reprinted from *Beyond this Place There Be Dragons: The routes of the tragic trek of the Death Valley 1849ers through Nevada, Death Valley, and on to Southern California* by George Koenig, The Arthur Clark Company

"found water ... no grass." It is probable that Haynes was referring to water found around the edges of alkaline lake beds that can be palatable for the desperate.

Death Valley '49ers   31

By now, the notion that the parties were all family, burdens were to be shared, and the weak were to be aided had given way to the instinct for survival. William Manly was a notable exception to this. His ability to forage on his own and his survival skills were superior to the others and they relied on him for scouting ahead, which he routinely did. Spending many days and nights on foot alone and apart from the increasingly laboring wagon train, he had time to wrestle with thoughts of moving ahead on his own:

> "Prospects now seemed to me so hopeless, that I heartily wished I was not in duty bound to stand by the women and small children who could never reach a land of bread without assistance. If I was in the position that some of them were who had only themselves to look after, I could pick up my knapsack and gun and go off, feeling I had no dependent one to leave behind. But as it was I felt I should be morally guilty of murder if I should forsake Mr. Bennett's wife and children and the family of Mr. Arcan with whom I had been thus far associated. It was a dark line of thought but I always felt better when I got around to the determination, as I always did, to stand by my friends, their wives and children let come what might."

Yucca Flat was visible to the west, but seeing snow on a mountain lying south in the distance (Mt. Charleston), they believed the route south following Nye Canyon provided better prospects to find water. Manly, the Bennett-Arcans, and the Nusbaumers moved south from Papoose Lake following the canyon on the eastern edge of the Test Site. Turning west through the pass into Frenchman Flat, just south of Control Point-1, they moved up through Cane Springs Wash. On the north side of Skull Mountain toward Jackass Flat, they found Cane Springs. Louis Nusbaumer would report in his diary that the parties stayed at Cane Springs for nine days. Here is Manly's description of coming upon a hut and Cane Springs, which he termed "the Indian farm":

Here was a flat place in a table land and on it a low brush hut. We approached carefully and cautiously, making a circuit around so as to get between the hut and the hill ... When within thirty yards, a man poked his head out of a doorway and drew it back again quick as a flash ... a child or two in the hut squalled terribly, fearing, I suppose, they would all be murdered ...

The poor fellow was shivering with cold. With signs of friendship we fired off one of the guns, which waked him up a little and he pointed to the gun and said "Walker," probably meaning the same good Chief Walker who had so fortunately stopped us in our journey down the Green River.

... By the aid of a warm spring near by they had raised some corn here, and the dry stalks were standing around.

Manly's description of a low brush hut is consistent with the

Cabin at Cane Springs, circa 1969 - Source: Archeological Investigation at the U.S. AEC's Nevada Test Site and Nuclear Rocket Development Station, Frederick C. Worman

fact that the stone structure currently at Cane Springs was not built until the late 1800's. The present structure consists of three adjoining cabins, one stone and two frame, and corrals built to hold relay horses for a stage line that never operated and for a freight line that did (more on this later). As mentioned previously, the stone building contained a fireplace with the block inscribed with the name "F. O. BYOR" and the date "1847," two years before Manly and the other parties were there. There is no mention of the BYOR rock in either the Manly or Nusbaumer accounts of their stay at Cane Springs, but the rock is smallish, perhaps 14 inches long, and could easily have been missed.

The following passage describes Manly's and Rogers' departure from Cane Springs and provides some insight into the plight facing the parties:

> As we were about to leave I told him [*the Indian*] we would come back, next day and bring him some clothes if we could find any to spare, and then we shouldered our guns and went back toward the wagons, looking over our shoulders occasionally to see if we were followed. We walked fast down the hill and reached the camp about dark to find it a most unhappy one indeed. Mrs. Bennett and Mrs. Arcane were in heart-rendering distress. The four children were crying for water but there was not a drop to give them, and none could be reached before some time next day. The mothers were nearly crazy, for they expected the children would choke with thirst and die in their arms, and would rather perish themselves than suffer the agony of seeing their little ones gasp and slowly die. They reproached themselves as being the cause of all this trouble. For the love of gold they had left homes where hunger had never come, and often in sleep dreamed of the bounteous tables of their old homes only to be woefully disappointed in the morning. There was great gladness when John Rogers and I appeared in the camp and gave the mothers full canteens of water for themselves and little ones, and there was tears of joy and thankfulness upon their cheeks as they blessed us over and over again.

Abandonded Wagon, Cat & Fortymile Canyon - Roscoe Wright (Death Valley Curly) and Georgia Wheeler, circa 1940 - Source: Nevada Historical Society

The Jayhawkers, in small groups, left Papoose Lake beginning early December 2nd. They would set their own trail through the Test Site trekking along the waterless east side of Yucca Flat. Koenig concludes that after three days they went west in the direction of Tippipah Spring, but no mention was made of any spring and it seems likely they did not see it. This route took them to the northern end of Jackass Flat and the entrance to Fortymile Canyon. They followed Jackass Flat to the south and, to their misfortune, bypassed Cane Springs with its water and grass on the north side of Skull Mountain. Just south of the Test Site, in the Amargosa Valley, they followed the riverbed of the Amargosa in the area of Ash Meadows on their way to nearby Death Valley. Following in their track several days later were the Briers.

Juliet Brier – Across the NTS in '49

"Every step I take will be toward California." - Juliet Brier

By all accounts, Reverend James Welsh Brier's wife, Juliet (Julia) was a remarkable woman. William Manly wrote of her:

> Mr. and Mrs. Brier had some pretty hard struggles to get along, and every one of this party has ever been loud in praise of the energy and determination of the brave little woman of the Brier mess ... She was the one who put the packs on the oxen in the morning. It was she who took them off at night, built the fires, cooked the food, helped the children, and did all sorts of work when the father of the family was too tired, which was almost all of the time. . . Mrs. Brier had the sympathy of every one, and many would have helped her if they could ... It seemed almost impossible that one little woman could do so much. It was entirely due to her untiring devotion that her husband and children lived. . .

She earned the Jayhawker's great respect by nursing their sick and dying, and by her devotion to her family. After leaving the Test Site, she walked nearly a hundred miles through sand and rock, frequently carrying one of their children on her back and another in her arms. As told by Manly, by the nightmare journey's end she was assisting her husband, who had lost a hundred pounds during the three-month ordeal.

The Briers followed the Jayhawkers across the Test Site, but were days behind. They too missed Cane Springs, cutting west before sighting it. They continued through upper Jackass Flat and into a branch of Fortymile Canyon in the area of Tippipah Spring. In 1901, Juliet Brier recalled those days on the NTS.

> Our first serious troubles began when we arrived at what was apparently a big lake. Instead of water we found it to be merely glazed mud with a little alkali water. Three days later we reached a branch of Fortymile Canyon, where a foot of snow fell upon us. We stayed here a week to recuperate and our cattle suffered much from cold. Finding that the oxen would carry packs well the company loaded the necessaries on the cattle and burned everything else with the wagons. It was a fatal step as we were about 500 miles from Los Angeles with only our feet to take us there.

Although some have reported that the Brier's route took them into Fortymile Canyon, it seems unlikely. The canyon is deeply gutted and littered with boulders and rocks and is virtually impassable for wagons. But it is in the area of Fortymile Canyon that the Briers burned their wagons and loaded packs on the cattle. It appears the Briers continued to follow the Jayhawker trail south through Jackass Flat. They exited the Test Site into the Amargosa Desert and eventually reunited on Christmas day with the Jayhawkers at Travertine Springs (near the present day Furnace Creek Inn). Juliet Brier, recalling that Christmas, would recount the following in the December 25, 1898 edition of the *San Francisco Call*:

> I don't know how to tell you about our struggle through Death Valley in 1849-50 and the Christmas we spent amid its horrors. I never expected to say anything about it for a newspaper. I was the only woman in the party – Mr. Brier, and our three boys, Columbus, John and Kirke, the oldest being nine years, and the two young men, John and Patrick made up our "mess" as we called it.
>
> We reached the top of the divide between Death and Ash valleys [Ash Meadows] and, oh what a desolate country we looked down into. The next morning we started down. The men said they could

see what looked like springs in the valley. Mr. Brier was always ahead to explore and find water, so I was left with our three boys to help bring up the cattle. They expected to reach the springs in a few hours and the men pushed ahead. I was sick and weary and the hope of a good camping place was all that kept me up. Poor little Kirke gave out and I carried him on my back, barely seeing where I was going, until he would say, "Mother, I can walk now." Poor little fellow! He would stumble on a little way over the salty marsh and sink down crying, "I can't go any farther." Then I would carry him again, and soothe him as best I could.

Many times I felt I should faint, and as my strength departed I would sink on my knees. The boys would ask for water, but there was not a drop. Thus, we staggered on over the salty wastes, trying to keep the company in view and hoping at every step to come to the springs. Oh! Such a day! If we had stopped I knew the men would come back at night for us. But I didn't want to be thought a drag or hindrance.

Night came on and we lost all track of those ahead. I would get down on my knees and look in the star-light for the ox tracks and then we would stumble on. There was not a sound and I didn't know whether we would ever reach camp or not.

About midnight we came around a big rock and there was my husband at a small fire.

"Is this the camp?" I asked.

"No, it six miles farther," he said.

I was ready to drop and Kirke was almost unconscious, moaning for a drink. Mr. Brier took him on his back and hastened to camp to save his little life. It was three o'clock Christmas morning when we reached the springs [Travertine Springs in Furnace Creek]. I only wanted to sleep but my husband said I must eat and drink or I would never wake up. Oh! Such a horrible day and night!

We found hot and cold springs there and scrubbed and rested. That was a Christmas none could ever forget.

Music and singing? My, not! We were too far gone for that. Nobody spoke very much, but I knew we were all thinking of home back east and all the cheer and good things there. Men would sit looking into the fire or stand gazing away silently over the mountains, and it was easy to read their thoughts. Poor fellows! Having no

Reverend Brier, Juliet Brier, and their three sons, circa 1852

other woman there, I felt lonesome at times, but I was glad, too, that no other was there to suffer.

The men killed an ox, and we had a Christmas dinner of fresh meat, black coffee, and a little bread. I had one small biscuit. You see we were on short rations then, and didn't know how long we would have to make provisions last. We didn't know we were in California. Nobody knows what untold misery the morrow might bring so there was no occasion for cheer.

Fred Carr said to me that night. "Don't you think you and the children better remain here and let me send back for you?"

I knew what was in his mind. "No," I said, "I have never been a hindrance, I have never kept the company waiting, neither have my children, and every step I take will be towards California."

Years later, John B. Colton, a Jayhawker, would remark:

"That little woman was grit clear through. I can tell you, we are all proud to account her as one of our number."

The entire Brier family made it out of "the Shadow of the Valley of Death" and settled in the northern California city of Lodi, near Stockton. Two years later, in 1851, Reverend Brier became a founder of California Wesleyan College, which is now the University of the Pacific in Stockton. Juliet would live to be 99 years old and host several annual meetings of the surviving Jayhawker group.

William Lewis Manly - Epilogue

Manly reached the goldfields and tried mining, but was unsuccessful. Disappointed, he returned to Wisconsin, but in 1851 was back in San Francisco, this time by boat and overland through the Isthmus of Panama. Back to the goldfields, he was modestly successful at gold mining and ran a small store. In 1859, he settled near San Jose and married Mary J. Woods. Manly died in 1903 at age 83 and was buried beside his wife in Woodbridge, California (near Lodi). His book, which immortalized the trek of the Death Valley '49ers, was not a commercial success and he had difficulty in selling copies for their $2 price. After its publication, other '49ers provided proposed additions or corrections, but age and infirmities prevented Manly from ever producing a second edition.

Mining On The NTS

Prospector's Cave in Cat Canyon - Source: Anatomy of tne Nevada Test
Site, Frederick C. Worman, Los Alamos Scientific Laboratory

Although it is surrounded by productive mining districts,
mining on the Test Site provided, at best, modest economic re-
turns.

Kawich - Just off the NTS to the north of Pahute Mesa was the
Kawich mining district. The name commemorates Shoshone Chief
Kawich who lived nearby. The Kawich camp was founded in 1904,
shortly after gold was discovered in the area. The townsite was
known as Gold Reed after the company of that name that man-
aged the most significant properties in the district. The town grew

41

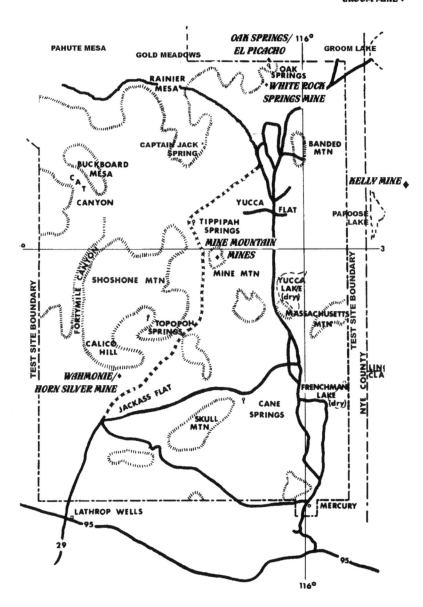

Mines in the area of the Nevada Test Site

Kawich (Gold Reed) circa 1930 - Source: Central Nevada Historical Society

to over 400 inhabitants with eight saloons, three stores, three restaurants, and three lodging tents. More than $10,000 worth of lots, ranging from $60 to $125, were sold. However, the nearest water was 15 miles, prompting one disgruntled visitor to say, "Kawich is a hell of a place. No mines, no water, no feed, and no women." From April 1905 until June 1908, a post office served the town, but did little business. Every now and then, an unscheduled stage line ran 70 miles northwest to Tonopah. A round-trip ticket cost $10. The gold ore, assayed at $35 per ton in one mine, rarely exceeded $10 per ton in the other mines and was soon uneconomical to transport. The site was abandoned in 1908. There was a revival of the Gold Reed mine in the 1940's, but all activity ceased when the land was purchased by the federal government for the Las Vegas Bombing and Gunnery Range.

Groom - Just off the Test Site, northeast in Lincoln County and now part of Area 51, was Groom Mine. Lead and silver were discovered there in 1864. Dr. Margaret Long, in *The Shadow of the Arrow*, writes that in 1866 there was an old, crude smelter on the property. She speculated that its origin may have been Spanish or Mormon, noting that the Mormons mined lead at Potosi, southwest of Las Vegas, in the 1850's. Captain Jack, for whom Captain Jack Spring in the Belted Range (Area 12) is named, carried mail over the pack trail from Utah to Groom. The main trail from Tickapah Spring to White Rock Spring passed north of Groom and is reported to have gone on to California. Captain Jack followed a branch trail along the east base of the Naquintas from Tickapah Spring to the Groom Mine. Captain Jack said one of the pack trails, over which he carried mail, was also used by white men who carried ore from Groom to Utah and traded it for provisions. The 1860's presence of Mormans in the area led Dr. Long to speculate that earlier Mormon presence, prior to 1850, may have some bearing on the origin of the "cutoff" myth that led the Death Val-

Groom Mine overlooking Groom Lake - Source: Beyond This Place There Be Dragons by Arthur Koenig, The Arthur H. Clark Company

Before the Nukes

ley '49ers astray.

The name "Groom" appeared in the early 1870's as a result of the financing of the Conception Mines by Groome Lead Mines Limited, an English firm. The area contained mostly low grade ores of silver and lead – no gold. Records show that $80,000 was spent on roads and development before the mine was abandoned five years later because it was too isolated. There were several owners of the property through the years. In 1917 through 1918, Groom was the second largest lead producer in Nevada. With the death of its owner, T. J. Osborn, the mine closed in 1918. In 1937, Groom Mine was acquired by the Sheehan Brothers who made sporadic attempts to operate the mine. Production resumed in earnest after World War II and continued after the opening of the Test Site. Throughout the period of atmospheric tests on the Test Site (1950's), the AEC was routinely forced to delay tests or evacuate those working the mine. Finally, in 1958, the AEC concluded it was in the best interests of the government to secure complete and absolute control of all the properties in the Groom Mine Area. Shortly thereafter, the government purchased the property.

Oak Spring – Oak Spring is just north of Yucca Flat. Claims were filed at Oak Springs as early as March, 1889. The Beatty Bullfrog Miner reported miners in the area in 1905. During this time, a miner named McClure had a claim of turquoise incorporated as the Turquoise Mining Company. Gold and silver occurred in several areas near Oak Spring. In 1917, a small quantity of copper ore containing a little silver was shipped from the Horseshoe claim. Hearing about the copper/silver prospect, Bud Cowan, then operating a stage line, organized the El Picacho mine. Cowan worked the mine during the years 1922-1928 with little success. It was his wife, B. M. Bower, who would use the quiet days spent in that desolate area for a different purpose. A detailed insight into her life and times on the Test Site is the subject of a later chapter. Tungsten exploration didn't occur until the latter part of the 1930's. The Climax tungsten mine, closed prior to nuclear testing, is a familiar location to many who worked on the Test Site. In June 1966, it was used as the site of the Pile Driver event, a 62 kiloton nuclear weapons effects test detonated in a tunnel 1518 feet underground in granite.

Pocopah – Copper, gold, silver, and magnesite were discovered in Fortymile Canyon in 1904 and the Pocopah Mining District was formed. Newspaper references in 1904-07 refer to claim activity in this district which is an area four miles by eight miles located on the east end of the Calico Range. It was described as west of the Wahmonie district and north of Jackass Flats, about six miles north of the Cane Springs road.

White Rock Springs – A relative latecomer, White Rock Springs, sometimes referred to as part of the Oak Springs mining district, was a silver mining area discovered in 1905. Very little work was done at that time, however there were reports of occasional activity at White Rock Springs until 1938.

Mine Mountain - The Mine Mountain Mining District, referred to on some maps as the Tippipah Spring Mining District, was formed in 1928, listing mercury, lead, silver, and antimony as the metals. The following is from Nevada Bureau of Mines and Geology Report No. 3090 0006:

> The mine workings on Mine Mountain consist of four shallow shafts, four adits[1] and several groups of prospect-pits and trenches. The

---

1 An opening driven horizontally into the side of a mountain or hill for providing access to a mineral deposit

46

Large mercury retort at Mine Mountain - Source: Lawrence Livermore National Laboratory

remains of two mercury retorts are also located on the eastern slopes of the mountain. One of these retorts is a makeshift arrangement below one of the eastern adits, the second is a masonry and pipe job, close to the main road into the district on the east side of the mountain. The presence of retorts suggests an attempt was made to mine and process mercury ore at some earlier time. There is, however, no record of mercury production from the district.

In 1982, the Nevada Bureau of Mines and Geology did 12 sample assays. Gold did not exceed .03 ounces per ton, but one sample assayed silver at 4 ounces per ton. *Undiscovered gold in the Mine Mountain area?* Perhaps, as the summary of this report notes:

Although gold was not anomalous in the limited sample set, a general model for a disseminated gold deposit clearly fits the lithologies, structures and geochemistry of Mine Mountain. Expanding the size of the study area in the same environment is strongly indicated.

Mining on the NTS   47

Bill McKinnis, former Lawrence Livermore National Laboratory employee, visited the Mine Mountain area (Test Site Area 6) on several occasions and observed:

> There is a foot trail from a main camp to five tunnels into the side of Mine Mountain. The longest tunnel is perhaps 40 feet. On the top of the mountain are three shafts, exact depth unknown, but relatively shallow. The southern most shaft is lined with one-inch boards and has a small concrete pad at the surface. The amount of work completed on the tunnels and shafts indicates a sizeable investment for the times – much more than a free-lance prospector could afford. Near the three shafts is a small mercury retort with charred support timbers. Based on the small size, it most likely was used for assaying cinnabar (mercuric sulfide), rather than for production of mercury. A nearby can dump contains hole-in-top (or hole-in-cap) cans.[1] By 1922 the replacement "sanitary can," an open top can crimped and soldered on the top rim, was in general use. Sanitary cans were also found along with the remains of the legs of an ironing board and a cook stove.
>
> McKinnis believes there were two mining periods on Mine Mountain, sometime before 1920 and sometime in the late 1920's or early 1930's, the latter date being consistent with NBMG records.

In the camp area are the remains of a two-hole outhouse. This, and the size of the tunnel, means that, at one time, there must have been a sizeable crew working the claim. McKinnis's examination of the large retort arouses suspicion about its intended use. Retorts are designed like a still with a pressure kettle and a coil. Mercury ore is heated inside the kettle, vaporizes and escapes through the coil, which condenses it into droplets that are collected in a mer-

---

1 Cans of this era were manufactured completely by hand and included a top with a one-inch circular hole through which the can was filled. After filling, a cap with a small vent hole was soldered over the opening. During the cooking process, steam would escape through the vent hole, which was then closed with a drop of solder.

cury flask. McKinnis noted that the metal kettle had never been sealed and could not have been used as a retort. Unlike the smaller retort, there were no signs that the retort had ever been heated. It is McKinnis's speculation that chicanery, not mercury, was the intended product. He poses that investors would be taken to the area, shown the production-sized tunnel, the shafts, and the large retort to entice them to invest in what would ultimately prove to be a worthless mine.

There are few records of the Mine Mountain Mining District and, by 1940, there is no evidence of activity in the area. A search of the Nye County Recorder's records by this author showed no claims filed for this area from 1920 to 1934.

Wahmonie - Wahmonie, located in Area 26, is the Test Site's quintessential boom-bust mining ghost town. S. H. Ball, USGS, reported mining on the edge of Jackass Flat before 1905, but since the finds were unremarkable, they were abandoned. In February of 1928, two prospectors, William McCrea and Mark Lefler, discovered high-grade silver-gold ore near where "the Mormons sank a 20 foot hole, a 10 foot hole and started a crosscut tunnel. They evidently found hornsilver on the surface, but the values quit them deeper down and they left. There are still standing the remnants of two old rock cabins." McCrea and Lefler, and others, were apparently aware that "the old Hornsilver Mine had been worked by Mormons in 1853." Their initial discovery was described as being "very near several old holes dug by Mormons in 1853 from which very rich horn-silver was extracted." Wahmonie lies near Cane Springs on the old Mormon Trail from Salt Lake City to San Bernardino, California. The stone found at Cane Springs with the inscription "F. O. BYOR, 1847," discussed previously, adds credence to the report of workings at the Hornsilver Mine prior to the discovery of gold in California in 1849.

File No. 17169
Buckhorn
Cane Spring Mining District.   CERTIFICATE OF LOCATION.

THE UNDERSIGNED, hereby certify that they have located a mining claim in the Cane Springs Mining District, County of Nye, State of Nevada, on a vein or lode, known as the Buckhorn. The general course of said lode or vein, as near as it may be described, is Northerly and Southerly. The names of the locators Mark Lefler and W.R.McCrea. The said claim was located on the 31st day of January 1928, and is described in respect to natural object as 4½ miles westerly from Cane Springs and end lines the Cane Springs lode on the South and Jumbo Fraction lode on the west. The locators claim 750 feet in length along the course of said vein or lode each way from the point of discovery with a width of 300 feet on each side of the center of the vein or lode along the entire length of said claim.

The dimensions and location of the discovery shaft work is shaft 4 x 6 x 10 feet deep located about 400 feet southerly of the location monument, and the location and description of each corner with the markings thereon are as follows:

The northwest corner is marked by a rock monument 3 feet high, inscribed N.W. corner of Buckhorn lode mine, the southwest corner is marked by a rock monument 3 feet high inscribed S.W. corner of Buckhorn mine, the southeast corner is marked by rock monument 3 feet high, inscribed S.E. corner Buckhorn mine, the Northeast corner is marked by a rock monument 3 feet high, inscribed N.E. corner Buckhorn mine. There is a rock monument marking each side center at each corner of each line. The discovery work has been done and the location work completed since Feb. 26, 1928.

Dated Wahmonie Feb. 26, 1928/
                                            Mark Lefler
                                            W.R.McCrea

Recorded at Request of W.R.McCrea Feb. 28th, 1928 at 9 o'clock A.M. in Volume A of Wahmonie page ___39___ County Records.
                              Jos.D.O'Brien - Recorder.   (Seal)

Filed for record at request of George Wingfield March 1, 1928 at 47 minutes past 11 o'clock A.M.

Nye Counter Recording of the Lefler and McCray "Buckhorn" mining claim dated Wahmonie February 26, 1928

A survey and sampling of the McCrae and Lefler claims by William Sharp in February 1928 noted a "high grade" area with 8.92 oz. gold and 314 oz. silver per ton. His conclusion:

On the whole, this is the best prospect I have seen for a long time and I recommend that the work be done on the main strike. It may dig out but if it improves it will certainly be worth while.

Postcard, Wahmonie, Nevada - Source: University of Nevada Las Vegas, Special Collections

Word of the discovery spread quickly and within three weeks over 200 miners and builders were at the site. Soon others arrived hauling small houses on trucks or in cars loaded with grub, lumber, tents, and stoves. The *Las Vegas Age* newspaper headlined "NEW WAHMONIE GOLD STRIKE OVERSHADOWS THE CRIPPLE CREEK STRIKE SAY OLD TIMERS" and went on to report "free gold in generous quantities can be seen plainly with the naked eye." Other newspaper articles enticed the adventurous to seek their fortune noting, "Former knowledge and experience is of little value. Any tenderfoot who has the ambition to get out at 5 a. m. in the cold, and hustle into the mountains and has luck enough to get a claim is liable to have his made right now." The townsite blossomed with tents. Boarding houses opened, tent stores sold dry goods and cafes offered ham, eggs, and coffee for a dollar. Within weeks, over 1,000 claims had been staked as the miners continued to pour into Wahmonie. The Wahmonie Mining District was established February 12, 1928; however, many filed claims referred to the Cane Springs (or Kane Springs) Mining District and this was dutifully recorded by the Nye County Recorder. A road to Wahmonie from Las Vegas was proposed, the Gold Bar Club and Restaurant was opened, and there were plans for a movie and dance hall. Accelerated by wildly optimistic reports of rich finds, the town reached its peak population of about 1,500 in April 1928.

On April 2, 1928 a post office was opened and pioneer residents requested air mail service. The Gilbert Brothers, who operated a groceries and supply tent, installed an electric light plant. In a surprise move, George Wingfield, Nevada's top mine and cattle operator, purchased the mine and claims from McCrea and Lefler. Shortly thereafter, he organized the Wahmonie Mine Company and developed the Hornsilver Mine. The Hornsilver Mine drove a

Gilbert Brothers Groceries & Supplies, Wahmonie, 1928 - Source: Nevada Historical Society

Hornsilver Mine headframe - Source: University of Nevada Reno, Special Collections

shaft to 500 feet, but only minor shipments were made and as ore values dropped to $3 a ton, the prevailing optimism faded. By the end of 1928, the town was a bust. Only a handful of people remained and the town was completely abandoned in 1931. I found structural remains, head frames, auto parts, sinks, and stoves during my several visits in 1960. Even the streets of the town were clearly visible at that time.

From 1921 to 1942, Dr. Margaret Long, a physician from Denver and the daughter of a governor of Massachusetts, made several trips into the area of the Nevada Test Site. While there, she collected materials for her book, "The Shadow of the Arrow," which chronicled the trip of the Death Valley '49ers. The travels of this adventurous lady are discussed further in the chapter on *Trails, Roads, and Rails.* In 1928, Dr. Long and friends, Anne Martin, Charley Brown, and his young son, George, drove their "Studies" (Studebaker automobiles) to the then bustling town of Wahmonie. She describes the trip:

We turned off in the opposite direction [from Beatty and Tonopah] toward Wahmonie, a new gold camp. The road wound up through the sands of Tonopah Wash for some miles. Washes offer the path of least resistance over the rough surface of the desert. Automobile tires soon make two firm tracks which wind through the sand, and these tracks endure until the next cloudburst. We overtook another ancient dry-land mariner in bedroll, and washtub, he had left Beatty the day before to join the gold rush to Wahmonie. He told us he had broken camp at two in the morning in order to hurry on and get water for his mules. And it is but a few hours' ride from Beatty by automobile! When we poured the water we carried on the running board into his washtub for the thirsty mules he asked us if we hadn't some whiskey for a thirsty man and loudly lamented the fact that we had not.

Wahmonie was a town of tents along a single street. The mining activity was short-lived, and it has since then become a ghost town. The first tent bore a large sign reading "The Silver Dollar Saloon." It would have been boldly flaunted in the faces of the rampart votaries of Volstead[1] had any of them been present in this isolated camp. We had dinner, not at the Silver Dollar, but at the Northern Club; then we went to Cane Spring, four miles east. This spring supplies Wahmonie with water, but it is hauled, not piped. Near the spring are a roofless house, a tree, and a grave. The latter is marked by a headboard with the wording, "PETE BLACK, 1922," roughly cut into it. Whitey Bill, a member of the Mesquite Club, whom we met sometime afterwards, told us that he found Pete Black dead in his blankets one evening when he arrived at the spring with his mules. Pete had been dead for several days, so Bill camped some distance from the house. The sheriff was summoned and performed the obsequies.

It appears Dr. Long did not spend much time in Wahmonie, for she surely would have known of and perhaps met Clyde Forsythe, noted painter of western art turned prospector. Forsythe's prospecting adventures and Wahmonie paintings are discussed next.

---

[1] Referring to those devoted to the Volstead Act (National Prohibition Act) effected Jan. 1920 and not repealed until Dec. 1933.

Clyde Forsythe

One of the most interesting visitors to Wahmonie was (Victor) Clyde Forsythe (1885-1962), a painter of western landscapes. He was already nationally famous as the creator of cartoons and a comic strip, and he had painted several popular World War I posters.

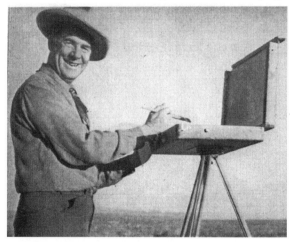

Clyde Forsythe - Source: Desert Magazine, photo by Ted Slocum

Forsythe was friends with Will Rogers and Norman Rockwell and had introduced Rockwell to the *Saturday Evening Post.* Forsythe immersed himself in the lore of the West and often lived in ghost towns while on painting forays. One such foray was to Wahmonie in February 1928. Forsythe stumbled onto the early stages of the Wahmonie boom by accident. He had set out for the Nevada desert with his wife, Cotta, to restock his sketchpad with new scenes to be used in future paintings. Refueling and stocking up on supplies, Forsythe had stopped at "a wide place in the road - Las Vegas." As he gassed up his Franklin sedan, he spotted a shabby little man sitting by the Coca Cola vending machine. The man, with a few weeks stubble on a well-tanned face, intrigued Forsythe. It was apparent to Forsythe that he had come across a real-life desert rat. He asked the man if he knew where there were any burros to paint. "If there's any burros around, they'll all be out to Wahmonie at the strike ... you ain't heard of the strike? Big strike, two weeks old, got a camp, miners staking out; we're in for grub and headin' back t'night." The man's name was George Davis and he was 72. Davis gave Forsythe the simple directions to Wahmonie: follow the road to Beatty for 90 miles, then look for a white rag on a stick in a bush, and follow a sandy wash for 20 miles. Wheel tracks would lead to the camp in the hills.

Fortifying his supplies with food, Forsythe was off for the hills. Once off the road to Beatty (now Highway 95), the going was slow because the wash was sand. Abandoned vehicles dotted the way. The Franklin crawled toward the camp. In the distance, plumes of smoke from burning piles of creosote bush marked the location on the slope of the shallow valley at the end of Jackass Flat. A few streets had been laid out and a dozen tents, including a grocery tent and a café tent, lined the main street. In Forsythe's own words:

We parked in the greasewood a couple of hundred yards from the camp and walked back to look for our little man, George Davis. He was there with his partner, Jim Ryan - two desert rats with several weeks of stubble on their tanned faces.

Davis and Ryan had a shabby little pup-tent in the center of "town." They had a pot of mulligan stew on the fire.

Human pride is where you find it - like gold. Dried-up little George Davis was the oldest man in camp. He had been honored by the men who know how to honor a man. They had named the highest peak in the range, "Mount Davis." We found that we were with a man of distinction! Ryan, the partner, was a young punk of my own age, 41.

Back to camp and the café. A 1x12 plank about 10 feet long served as a table. Ham and eggs and coffee at one dollar per person - but this was better than slavery over a campfire. Liquor too! A five gallon demijohn of gin, and one tumbler for all customers.

Before the Nukes

Then the gold bug bit Forsythe. Davis and Ryan came up with a most astonishing proposal: Forsythe should stake a claim.

A crap game in front of the Wahmonie Cafe - inspiration for a similar scene in "The Mining Camp" - Source: Desert Magazine

Forsythe's brother-in-law, Harold Gay, a mining engineer in Mexico was called to the site, and a claim was staked for him too. Real estate in Wahmonie was being subdivided and the Forsythes procured a lot for $170 - "a fine business corner where Jack Rabbit Lane intersects Broadway, not far from Dry Placer Gulch." In subsequent years, Forsythe would take a lot of good-natured ribbing about this purchase. When Gay arrived at Wahmonie, he and Forsythe walked the claims end to end for several hours, taking samples. The ore samples they extracted were sent to Los Angeles, where they assayed at 25¢ to the ton in gold - "Not rich enough to pay for the shoe leather we used in picking them up!"

While in Wahmonie, Forsythe spent a few hours sketching studies of the camp. This was Forsythe's Wahmonie legacy, not defined by gold, but rather by his series of four paintings titled *The Gold Strike* which he produced from the sketches. The initial painting, done in 1938, was titled *The Gold Rush*. One year later, Forsythe produced three additional paintings, *The Mining Camp*, *The Mining Town*, and *The Ghost Town*. *The Mining Camp* (cover) shows life in Wahmonie centered around the Gilbert Brothers' grocery tent. The final painting in the series, *The Mining Town*, was Forsythe's idea of how Wahmonie might have looked had it actually been

The Mining Town by Clyde Forsythe · Source: Desert Magazine

another Goldfield.

Unfortunately, I have been unable to locate any of the original paintings of *The Gold Strike* series. In 1960, *Desert Magazine* (now defunct) made lithographs of them and they are shown on the next page. While researching *The Gold Strike* series, I came across another Forsythe painting, *Mining Camp in High Mojave Desert*, which is on display in the law offices of Goold Patterson Ales & Day in Las Vegas. Although not one of *The Gold Strike* series, it bears a striking resemblance to an early photo of Wahmonie. This author and the painting's owner, Barry Goold, have concluded that it is a painting of Wahmonie. Judge for yourself by comparing the photo and painting (page 60) to see if you agree. For a view of this painting (and other classic western paintings) displayed in color, visit www.gooldpatterson.com.

Before the Nukes

Clyde Forsythe's The Gold Strike Series

The Gold Rush

The Mining Camp

The Mining Town

The Ghost Town

Another Forsythe painting of Wahmonie

Mining Camp in the High Mojave Desert by Clyde Forsythe - Courtesy of Barry and Lynda Goold Family Trust

Wahmonie Panorama - Source: Nevada Historical Society

B. M. Bower

It's hard to imagine a woman living at Oak Springs on the north end of the Test Site in the 1920's. What makes this story even more remarkable is that she was a famous author of the times. Much of story of B. M. Bower's days on the Test Site is taken from "El Picacho, The Writing Cabin of B. M. Bower" by Alvin R. McLane.

B. M. Bower (1871-1940) was a prolific writer of Western fiction. Born Bertha Muzzy in Cleveland, Minnesota, she moved to Montana with her parents at the age of seventeen. Bert, as she preferred to be called, spent many hours on ranches, visiting with cowboys. She was married three times to working cowboys. The first marriage, in 1890, was to Clayton Bower under whose name she wrote the rest of her life. Bertha masked her gender by using

B. M. Bower, c. 1920 - Source: Estate of B. M. Bower, courtesy of Kate B. Anderson

her initials, B. M., because her publishers did not think that her novels would be a commercial success if readers knew that the

B. M. Bower's writing cabin at El Picacho Mine in 1920s - Source - Estate of B. M. Bower, courtesy of Kate B. Anderson

writer was a woman. The Bowers divorced in 1905. Later that year, she married Bertrand Sinclair with whom she had been a friend for a number of years. The marriage lasted until 1911, but during that time she helped Sinclair become a successful writer of western and Canadian literature. Her third marriage was to Bud Cowan in 1920. Among other occupations, Cowan had a short-lived stage route and mail contract between Caliente and Pioche, Nevada. It was Cowan who had heard of the Oak Spring copper/silver prospect. Bower liked the idea of a quiet spot on the desert to write, and the possibility that money might be made from a producing silver mine. The couple moved to Nevada in 1920 and took up residence at Oak Springs. Together they formed the El Picacho Mining Company, Inc., with Bower as president. Those who have worked on the Test Site can well appreciate the desolation of the area at a time when roads were virtually non-existent. Bower her-

El Picacho Mine site in the 1920s - Source: Estate of B. M. Bower, courtesy of Kate B. Anderson

self notes how interesting a shopping list is for such an isolated area. She writes, "My last shopping, for instance, included dynamite, carbon paper, detonating caps, messaline, fuse, the latest magazines, a new typewriter, and half the innards of a Ford."

Before the Bowers, many others had worked the area, with claims filed as early as 1889. Gold and silver occurred in the quartz veins 1.5 miles south of Oak Spring. Turquoise, gold, and silver were found at other locations nearby. In 1917, a small quantity of copper ore containing a little silver was shipped from the Horseshoe claim. It was probably this shipment that prompted Cowan and Bower to organize the El Picacho Mining Company.

Letters of Bower indicate that they resided at El Picacho from 1920 to 1926, with a short stay in 1928. There were two main houses of stone with corrugated iron roofs. Bower had a cabin by herself where she did her writing so nobody could bother her. The cabin measures thirty-five by twenty-four feet. In the near vicinity are a root cellar, rock retaining walls, and a privy. It was here, during this time, that Bower wrote eleven novels. They were *Casey Ryan*, *The Trail of the White Mule*, *The Eagle's Wing*, *The Voice at Johnnywater*, *The Parowan Bonanza*, *The Bellehelen Mine*, *Desert Brew*, *Black Thunder*, and three stories set with a Montana background – *Meadowlark Basin*, *Van Patten*, and *White Wolves*. Johnny Water (Jonnies Water) and Bellehelen Mine are real places in the Belted and Kawich ranges just off the Test Site.

After the El Picacho period, Bower and Cowan moved to Las Vegas. Bud Cowan was elected Las Vegas Marshal (equivalent to today's chief of police) for that city in 1925. Later making their home in the artists' colony of Sierra Madre near Los Angeles, they continued working the El Picacho Mine sporadically over the next few years. Bud Cowan died in Las Vegas in 1938. B. M. Bower died in 1940 leaving a legacy of 68 novels, more than a dozen of which were made into movies. Some featured famous western stars, including Hoot Gibson and Tom Mix. Even with her passing, few of her readers knew that this western novelist was a woman.

Trails, Roads, and Rails

Prior to 1847, the only trails through the Test Site were those known to the local Native Americans between watering places. A Nevada Bureau of Mines and Geology report on the Wahmonie Mining District noted that the old Mormon Trail from Salt Lake to San Bernardino included Groom, Oak Spring, Tippipah Spring, Kane (Cane) Springs, and Wahmonie. In 1846, President James K. Polk requested Mormons to assist the U. S. Army during the Mexican War. The Mormon Battalion of 500 men was formed and moved to California to serve as a home guard for settlers. In 1847, a portion of the Battalion returning to Utah from San Diego may well have passed through the Test Site. This and other events discussed later in this chapter led to speculation by Dr. Margaret Long and others that the F. O. BYOR stone found at Cane Springs, dated 1847, may have been carved by one of the Mormon Battalion members.

Tonopah to Kawich auto stages, circa 1910 - Source: Central Nevada Historical Society

The age of motor travel began in 1903, when Horatio Nelson Jackson with his mechanic, Sewell Crocker, drove his Winton Motor Carriage from San Francisco to New York. At the time, there were no paved roads, save for a few miles in large cities. With countless repairs, tire replacements, and difficulty in obtaining gasoline, the trip took 63 days, but changed the way America would travel. Within two years, the richness of the silver load in Tonopah, Goldfield, and the surrounding area hastened the advent of the car to the southern Nevada desert. In 1905, the Nevada Mobile Transit Company operated 12 autos from Las Vegas to Rhyolite and on to Goldfield, a total distance of 194 miles. The route connected Goldfield to the Los Angeles-Salt Lake rail stop at Las Vegas. By 1906, the automobile was a routine sight in towns like Beatty, Rhyolite, Goldfield, and Tonopah. During the boom times in Tonopah and Goldfield, there were no major ore strikes in the area of the Test Site and it remained relatively devoid of cars. The accompanying USGS map, which is dated 1910 but surveyed in 1905-06, shows the "road" system crossing the area of the NTS. The term "road" is used loosely, as these were unmaintained trails that gave the traveler a passable way to get through the mountains and across the desert. In those times, traveling on the desert, outside the relatively comfortable boomtowns, was still best left to those who were hearty and well schooled in survival on the desert. This is clearly attested to by Robert H. Chapman, USGS, who, after traveling the area of the NTS in 1906, had this sage advice to fellow travelers:

> The traveler in the deserts should be sound in heart, kidneys, and liver; have calm judgment; obtain all information possible of watering places before undertaking a journey; never leave camp without some food and water; discount from 30 percent to 50 percent the physical efficiency of himself and his animals as experienced in other, cooler, fields, and abstain from alcoholic drinks, especially when doing physical labor. Many cases of collapse and death are due to alcohol

Before the Nukes

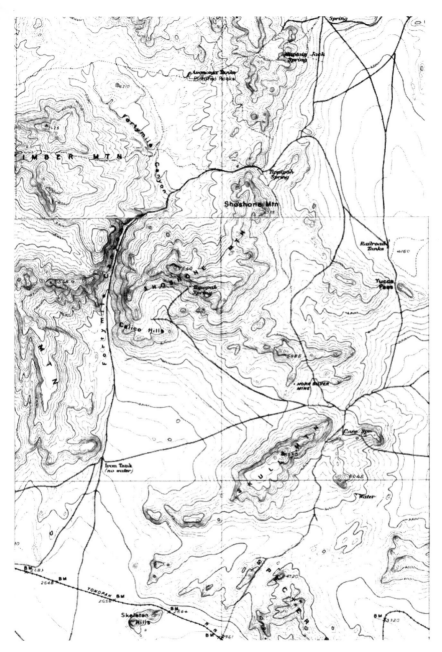

Roads in the area of the NTS circa 1906 - Source: USGS Furnace Creek
and Kawich Quandrangle maps, 1910

or overestimation of strength.

One of the first to provide a comprehensive record of motor travel in the area of the NTS was Dr. Margaret Long. Dr. Long's father was governor of Massachusetts from 1880 to 1882 and Secretary of the Navy during the McKinley and Roosevelt administrations. She earned her medical degree from Johns Hopkins Medical

School and practiced in Denver, Colorado. During 1921 to 1942 Dr. Long made frequent trips to the Death Valley region where she collected information for her book, *The Shadow of the Arrow*, first published in 1941, chronicling the trek of the Death Valley 49ers.

In 1928, in her quest to research the route of the Death Valley 49ers, Dr. Long made her first "entrada" into the area of the NTS to locate "Last Camp," as the 49er's called it. It was a two-car ex-

Dr. Margaret Long - Source: The Shadow of the Arrow, The Claxton Printers, Inc.

pedition with her and Anne Martin[1] in their "Studie" and friend

Charley Brown and his son, George, in another "Studie." She described the trip as "but a few hours' ride from Beatty by automobile." They traveled on Highway 5 and then off the highway through Jackass Flat to Wahmonie, stopping at Cane Springs to fill their radiators and bottles. It was there they met two sunburned prospectors arriving in a topless Ford. Charley Brown hailed one of them as "Judge," introducing him as an eminent lawyer who had

---

[1] Anne Martin was a candidate for the U.S. Senate in 1920 and leader of the Women's Suffrage Movement in Nevada

Before the Nukes

Dr. Margaret Long (driver) and Anne Martin (front passenger), circa 1920
Source: National Woman Suffrage Association, U. S. Senate campaign

dispensed justice at Rhyolite before that town became a ghost city, twenty years earlier. The Judge provided them with helpful directions to Groom Lake. Dr. Long writes:

> So we went a few miles east to Frenchman's Flat and turned north through the Joshua trees on the gentle slope of Yucca Pass to Emigrant Valley. Our cars followed the shore of Tippipah Lake, an expanse of tawny sand rather than water. Once we approached a band of wild horses, but they tossed their heads and thundered away in a cloud of dust. At the fork to Oak Spring we turned in the opposite direction, eastward. After a mile or two we crossed a slight rise in the valley and saw our goal, Groom Dry Lake.
>
> The buildings of the Groom Mine are above the lake on the southern tip of the Naquinta Mountains. As we approached we saw windows lighted by the setting sun and hoped that empty houses were not mocking us with a false welcome. We found they were not. The Sheehan family [*owners of the Groom Mine*] was waiting with true desert hospitality to welcome strangers whose car they had watched emerging from the mysterious distance across the great dry

lake. They provided a fine supper, during which we listened to the radio. Across the same wilderness through which exhausted emigrants had steered this chartless course in 1849 came a distant discussion of the Boulder Dam bill from the Senate in Washington.

Dr Long's next trip into the area of the NTS was made in 1937 when she and her brother went with Charley Brown in search of the springs mentioned by the Forty-niners.

It was a lonely region, visited occasionally by prospectors and cattlemen. In the hundred-mile drive from the highway (US 95), across Emigrant Valley to Crystal Spring in Pahranagat Valley, we met not another automobile. The unimproved road which goes north from the state highway junction called Rose's Well divides after the first mile. One fork up Fortymile Canyon is practically impassable. The other fork winds northeast, up the sands of Topopah Wash, east of Fortymile. We ascended the latter fork for several miles and turned east, away from the wash towards Wahmonie. The camp has so completely disappeared that Wahmonie cannot even be called a ghost city.

In 1938, Dr. Long visited the area twice in attempts to locate more springs that might have been associated with the Forty-niners. The first trip was again with Anne Martin, Charley Brown, and Herman Jones, whom she describes as a pilot familiar with the region. The details of the trip are sketchy, but being low on oil for the automobile they were forced to leave the Emigrant Valley area to head back to Shoshone. Heading south, they struck the Beatty-Las Vegas highway near the ghost railroad station of Charleston.

The wooden building has vanished completely, and the railroad grade, which used to serve as an automobile road after the tracks of the Las Vegas and Tonopah Railroad were taken up, has been abandoned for the new oiled highway [then Nevada Highway 5, now US 95].

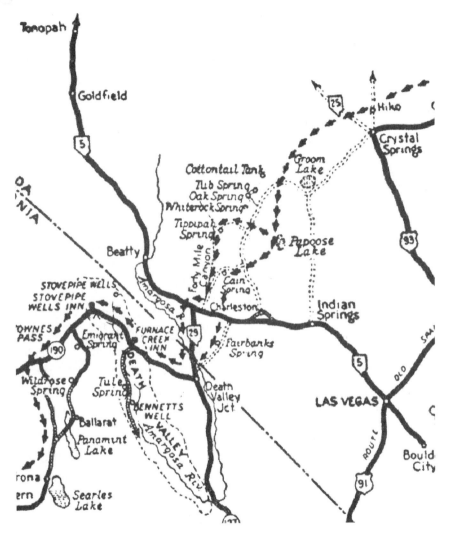

1940's road map used by Dr. Margaret Long - Source: The Shadow of the Arrow, The Claxton Press, Ltd.

In late May, 1938, Dr. Long and Anne Martin returned to the Emigrant Valley area with Whitey Bill, a cattleman and prospector.

Whitey Bill related that in 1920, he and another man drove a Model T Ford up Fortymile Canyon almost reaching Tippipah Spring before the steep ascent forced them to turn back. After visiting Tub Spring, Oak Spring, White Rock Spring, and Tippipah Spring, they again reached "the oil" (oiled Highway 5, now Highway 95). After that trip, Dr. Long would remark, "We can hardly blame them [*the Death Valley '49ers*] for missing so many of the springs in the surrounding mountains."

Dr. Long's last trip was in 1940, just prior to the closing of the area by the Army Air Corps to form the Las Vegas Bombing and Gunnery Range. On that trip, she crisscrossed the area several times, guided, in part, by a map from the U.S. War Department and signs that had been erected in the intervening years. Her log, short and cryptic, noted several signs to the Kelly Mine at various crossroads and other signs pointing the way to Oak Spring, Tippipah Spring, and White Rock Spring. She again visited Cane Springs, but only mentioned that Wahmonie was four miles distant. By this time, she knew the Emigrant Valley locals well. Bill Smith, manager of the Kelly Mine, and his wife only came in the summers as did the Sheehans, owners of Groom Mine. However, Dr. Long's log of that trip does not mention where she stayed or of seeing the Smiths or Sheehans. The roadmap used by Dr. Long on this last trip to the area of the NTS is shown on the previous page.

Las Vegas and Tonopah Railroad

Few motorists and Test Site workers realize that much of their trip from Las Vegas to the Test Site on Highway 95 is on the subgrade of the first railroad to reach the gold fields from the south – the Las Vegas and Tonopah Railroad.

Construction began on the Las Vegas and Tonopah Railroad

Las Vegas & Tonopah Railroad, first excursion train to Beatty, October 1906 - Source: Central Nevada Historical Society

in December 1905. Senator William A. Clark of Montana and his brother, J. Ross Clark, financed the entire venture, having a fortune estimated to be in excess of $100,000,000, made primarily from copper mining in Montana. The Clarks were in competition for the routes to the rich mining districts of Tonopah and Goldfield. Two other railroads, the Bullfrog Goldfield and the Tonopah and Tidewater, were equally determined to be the major railroad connection to haul ore and passengers.

Senator Clark was a partner in the Salt Lake Route, which ran from Salt Lake City to Los Angeles, passing through Las Vegas. At the time, Las Vegas was a tent camp, just then turning into a town. Senator Clark judiciously avoided committing to building the line all the way to Tonopah and in October 1907, the Las Vegas and Tonopah line was terminated in Goldfield. Freight and passengers had to use the Tonopah and Goldfield line as the final leg to Tonopah. In March 1906, the first regular Las Vegas & Tonopah train operation began. It only ran as far as Indian Springs, a distance of 43 miles at an overall speed of 18 m.p.h. By March 1907, the first Pullman service was inaugurated between Los Angeles and Rhyolite. Unfortunately, the 1907-08 era was the peak year for business on the Las Vegas & Tonopah and the only year it

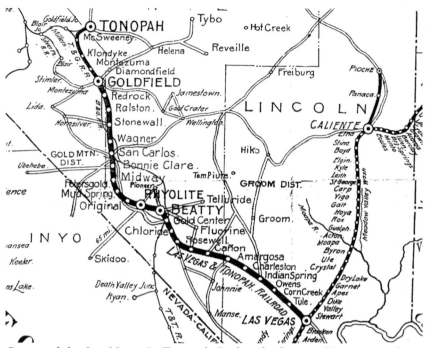

Route of the Las Vegas & Tonopah Railroad - Source: University of
Nevada Las Vegas, Special Collections

made money. After that, mining went into a slump and the 196
mile permanent rail line became a liability. By 1917, operating rev-
enues approximated only $8,000 per month with passengers num-
bering about eight on each train. Senator Clark decided to call it
quits and on October 31, 1918, the Las Vegas & Tonopah ceased
operations. The rails were pulled up and sold as scrap to support
the war effort. Nevada Highway 5 (now Highway 95) was built on
the abandoned right-of-way of the LV&T Railroad between Beatty
and Las Vegas. As the map shows, the LV&T Railroad never really
served the area of the Test Site. The nearest stops were well offsite
at Indian Springs, Charleston, Amargosa, and Rosewell (Rose's
Well). The Charleston stop is not near the present-day road to Mt.
Charleston. It was beyond Indian Springs in an area closer to the
intersection of the current Mercury Highway and US 95.

Before the Nukes

Formation of the Nevada Test Site

In 1940, with war looming on the horizon, the United States began a major rearmament program. Part of the program involved locating bombing and gunnery training ranges for the Army Air Corps. On October 29, 1940, President Franklin D. Roosevelt established the Las Vegas Bombing and Gunnery Range. The three and a half million acres north and west of Las Vegas stretched almost to Tonopah and included what is now the NTS. Most of the range was public domain, but condemnation proceedings were necessary to acquire the few homesteads and mining claims. These proceeding were completed in 1941. The Army Air Corps decided to use the range for an aerial gunnery school. The area currently encompassing the Test Site was to serve as a setting for air-to-air gunnery practice. Gunners used frangible bullets that broke upon impact, spattering paint so that gunners could see where their bullets had hit. Live fire was used against targets towed by other planes and the hazards of this, especially for the tow planes, fostered a requirement for emergency landing strips. Two of these were located in the area of the Test Site, one on Groom Lake, east of the site, and another on Pahute Mesa. The dry lake beds at Frenchman and Yucca Flats also served as emergency landing strips. At this time, the Army also established the base and landing strip at Indian Springs. At the end of the Second World War, training activities were closed out and the base at Las Vegas was deactivated. It remained in that state until 1948 when it was reopened as the Las

Vegas Air Force Base as part of a build up relating to the growing cold war threat. In 1950, the base was renamed Nellis Air Force Base.

By 1947, the Cold War had intensified. The nation's nuclear stockpile consisted of only 13 weapons, none of them assembled. Los Alamos had made advances that would theoretically improve the use of weapons-grade fissionable materials, then in short supply, but only testing could verify the designs. The Enewetak atoll in the Marshall Islands was decided upon for Operation Sandstone. After Sandstone, issues of weather, logistics, and security prompted the Atomic Energy Commission to create a task force, code-named Project Nutmeg, to investigate the feasibility of a continental test site. Headed by Navy Captain Howard Hutchinson, a "highly qualified meteorologist," the task was to determine "how, when, and where" tests could be conducted without "physical or economic detriment to the population." The search considered sites along the east coast where the prevailing winds would "blow the radioactivity harmlessly out to sea." The desert southwest was considered as having sites remote from population areas so that tests could be conducted "during two-thirds of the year, fully 40% of the time, in perfect safety." Nevada, Arizona, and New Mexico "offered optimum conditions as to meteorology, remote available land and logistics." New Mexico was the most logical choice because it was "a state conditioned to nuclear work." Given the perceived problems with all candidate locations, in March 1949 the Atomic Energy Commission concluded that, excepting a national emergency, a continental test site was not desirable.

Such an emergency came in the form of the first Soviet nuclear test in August 1949, much sooner that most had predicted. That event was followed shortly after, in June 1950, when the communist North Koreans stormed across the 38th parallel into South Korea. These events fostered a renewed search for a continental

Before the Nukes

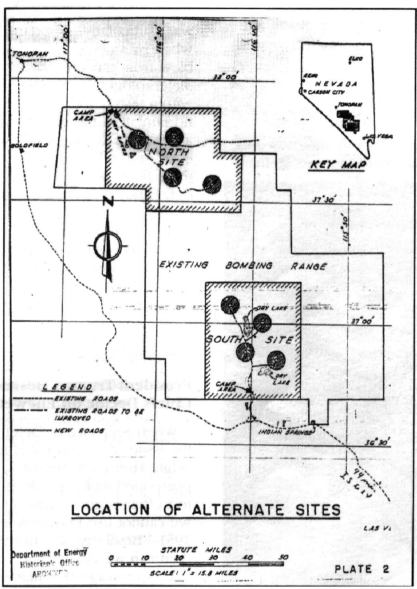

Holmes and Narver map showing the location of the North and South Sites - Source: Holmes and Narver, "Report covering the Selection of Proposed Emergency Proving Ground for the United States Atomic Energy Comission," August 14, 1950

test site, which was jointly undertaken by the Atomic Energy Commission and the Department of Defense. The choices narrowed to Dougway Proving Grounds in Utah, Alamogordo-White Sands in New Mexico, and two sites in Nevada on the Las Vegas Bombing and Gunnery Range. The North site was in the Goldfield-Tonopah area, and the South site was nearest Indian Springs. Assisting in the evaluation, Holmes and Narver determined that the South site had significant advantages over the North. Sources of material supplies were nearer and construction costs would be cheaper. Unlike the North site, the South site also had the advantage of natural screening barriers and permitted easier security enforcement.

Presented with the choices for a continental test site, President Truman postponed making a decision, instead requesting the National Security Council to lead the final search. Recognizing that a continental test site would not be available in time, a test series code-named Operation Greenhouse was planned for Enewetak in the fall of 1951. On December 18, 1950 at the urging of the Atomic Energy Commission and the Special Committee of the National Security Counsel, President Truman approved the choice of the South site for continental nuclear testing. Intensive planning was already underway at Los Alamos for a series of three to five shots to be conducted in mid-January or early February 1951. The series was code-named Ranger, and was a precursor to designs for tests in the upcoming Operation Greenhouse series. On January 27, 1951, at 5:45 a.m. a B-50D bomber dropped a nuclear device over Frenchman Flat. It exploded with a one-kiloton yield at a height of 1060 feet. This was the "Able" event that officially christened the Nevada Test Site and signaled the beginning of continental nuclear testing.

The Aftermath

"The adverse effects from indirect impacts [*i.e., site activities related to nuclear testing*] cannot be over emphasized. Most people have an innate curiosity about "antiquities," and many people are collectors to varying degrees. Employees of the Test Site and potential employees of the repository are no exception - many enjoy collecting artifacts. Often their impact is greater than the direct effects of a project."

Gregory H. Henton and Lonnie C. Pippin, August 1988

Able was not only the beginning of continental nuclear testing, it was also the beginning of a flood of tens of thousands of workers that would spill over the area of the NTS in the last 50 plus years. Free time would be spent by some roaming the furthest reaches of the NTS collecting mementos from historical sights. And with that, much valuable evidence of historical sites, historical artifacts, and previous inhabitants has all but disappeared. Congress, acknowledging this phenomenon, passed the 1966 National Historic Preservation Act noting:

"Historic properties significant to the Nation's heritage are being lost or substantially altered, often inadvertently, with increasing frequency."

The act went on further to mandate that:

It shall be the policy of the Federal Government, in cooperation with other nations and in partnership with the States, local governments, Indian tribes, and private organizations and individuals to

- administer federally owned, administered, or controlled

79

prehistoric and historic resources in a spirit of stewardship for the inspiration and benefit of present and future generations;

Long before National Historic Preservation Act mandates, preservation pioneers like Frederick C. Worman, Lonnie C. Pippin, William "Bill" McKinnis, and Don McGuffin preserved, as much as nature would allow, artifacts and records of some of the history of the area of the Test Site that surely would have been lost. The continuing efforts of those at the Department of Energy and the Desert Research Institute to both preserve and expand our knowledge of the history of the area of the Test Site can be found in the publications listed in the Bibliography.

Finally, where this book ends, the history of atomic testing begins, a history that has been chronicled in literally hundreds of books and thousands of documents. Fortunately, you will not have to read those thousands of documents because the atomic testing story is graphically depicted and well told by a visit to the **Atomic Testing Museum**, 755 East Flamingo Road, Las Vegas, Nevada. Their web site is **http://www.ntshf.org/**. This museum is a Smithsonian Institute affiliate and clearly done to Smithsonian standards. A walk through the museum is a walk through time, beginning with events leading up to the Manhattan Project. The *Ground Zero Theater* realistically mimics the sounds and feel of a nuclear test, from the viewpoint of an observer inside a concrete bunker. In addition to the origins and history of atomic testing, the *Stewards of the Land Gallery* includes showcases and exhibit panels on the archeology, endangered species, and Native American consultations. Spend some time here, as you will find displayed some of the artifacts and personalities mentioned in these pages. For those who would like to read more of the history of the Test Site, please review the Bibliography.

Index

Worman, Frederick C. 7
Wright, Roscoe C. 23

Y

Young, Sheldon 27
Yucca Flat 2
Yucca Mountain 12, 21

Bibliography

I. Unpublished Materials

Nye County Recorder's Office
Mining District Records, 1900 - 1938

II. Published Materials

A. Books and Periodicals

Brier, Rev. John Wells. *The Death Valley Party of 1849*. Out West, Vol XVIII, Nos. 3, 4, March-April 1903

Carah, Warren B. William Bowden Phillips: Early Pioneer of Mariposa County. Brighton, MI: 2003

Chapman, Robert H. *The Deserts of Nevada and Death Valley*. The National Geographic Magazine, Vol. XVII, No. 9, September 1906

Elliott, Russell R. *Nevada's Twentieth Century Mining Boom - Tonopah, Goldfield, Ely*. Reno: University of Nevada Press, 1966

Forsythe, Clyde. *How I Came to Paint "The Gold Rush."* Palm Desert, CA: Desert Magazine, June 1960

Forsythe, Clyde. *How I Came to Paint "The Mining Camp."* Palm Desert, CA: Desert Magazine, July 1960

Forsythe, Clyde. *How I Came to Paint "The Mining Town."* Palm Desert, CA: Desert Magazine, August 1960

Forsythe, Clyde. *How I Came to Paint "The Ghost Town."* Palm Desert, CA: Desert Magazine, September 1960

Grey, Dorothy. *Women of the West.* Lincoln and London: University of Nebraska Press, 1976

Hall, Shawn. *Preserving the Glory Days - Ghost Towns and Mining Camps of Nye County, Nevada.* University of Nevada Press, Reno and Las Vegas, 1981 & 1999

Koenig, George. *Beyond This Place There Be Dragons: The Routes of the Tragic Trek of the Death Valley 1849ers through Nevada, Death Valley, and on to Southern California.* Glendale, CA: The Arthur H. Clark Company, 1984

Las Vegas Age, various dates, 1928

Long, Dr. Margaret. *The Shadow of the Arrow.* Caldwell, Idaho: The Caxton Printers, Ltd., 1950

Manley, William Lewis. *Death Valley in '49.* New York, Santa Barbara, Wallace Hebberd, 1929

Manley, William L. *Death Valley in '49.* Santa Barbara, California: The Narrative Press, 2001

McBride, Terri. *Archeological Research in Nevada.* Carson City, Nevada: State Historic Preservation Office

McCracken, Robert D. *Modern Pioneers of the Amargosa Valley.* Tonopah, Nevada: Nye County Press, 1992

McLane, Alvin R. *El Picacho, The Writing Cabin of B. M. Bower.* Nevada Historical Society Quarterly, Vol. 39, No. 2, Summer 1996

Murbarger, Nell. *Ghosts of the Glory Trail.* Palm Desert, California: Desert Magazine Press, 1956

Myrick, David F. *Railroads of Nevada and Eastern California: Volume Two - The Southern Roads.* Berkeley, CA. Howell-North Books, 1963

Nusbaumer, Louis. *Valley of Salt, Memories of Wine.* Berkeley California: The Friends of the Bancroft Library, University of California. 1967

Stockton Daily Independent. *Julia Brier of Lodi is Dead.* Stockton, CA: May 27, 1913

Steward, Julian H. *Basin-Plateau Aboriginal Sociopolitical Groups.* Salt Lake City: The University of Utah Press

B. Maps

Nevada Test Site Relief Map, Department of Energy Nevada Operations Office, circa 2000

Kawich Quadrangle, U.S. Geological Survey, 1908

Furnace Creek Quadrangle, U.S. Department of Interior Geological Survey, 1910

Las Vegas Quadrangle, U.S. Department of Interior Geological Survey, 1908

Official Road Map of the State of Nevada, State of Nevada Department of Highways, 1937

Route of the Las Vegas & Tonopah Railroad

Nevada Test Site Areas, prepared by EG&G, January 1983

C. Department of Energy Publications

Dockery, Holly A., F.M. Byers Jr and Paul Orkild. *Nevada Test Site Field Trip Guidebook*, LA-10428-MS, Los Alamos, New Mexico: April 1985

Drollinger, Harold, Colleen Beck, and Robert Furlow. *Cultural Resources Management Plan for the Nevada Test Site*. DOE/NV 11508, June 1999

Drollinger, H., C. M. Beck, and R. C. Jones. *The Petroglyphs of Upper Fortymile Canyon Nevada Test Site Nye County Nevada, DOE/ NV/11508-50*, Las Vegas, Nevada: Desert Research Institute, January 1, 2000

Fehner, Terrence R. and F. G. Gosling. *Origins of the Nevada Test Site, United States Department of Energy*. History Division, Executive Secretariat, Management and Administration, Department of Energy, December 2000

Final Environmental Impact Statement for the Nevada Test Site and Off-Site Locations in the State of Nevada, DOE/EIS-0243, U.S. Department of Energy, Nevada Operations Office, Las Vegas, Nevada: 1997

Ford, Joe. *Wahmonie –NTS bonafide boom town*. Mercury, Nevada: *NTS News Bulletin*, August 21 & 28, 1981

Henton, Gregory H. and Lonnie C. Pippin. *Prehistoric and Historic Archeology of Fortymile Canyon, Yucca Wash, and Midway Valley near Yucca Mountain, Nye County, Southern Nevada*. Las Vegas, Nevada: Desert Research Institute, August 1988

NTS News & Views, U.S. Department of Energy, Nevada Field Office, Las Vegas, Nevada: April 1993

Worman, Frederick C. *Anatomy of the Nevada Test Site*. Los Alamos, New Mexico: Los Alamos Scientific Laboratory, March 1965

Worman, Frederick C. V. *Archeological Investigations at the U.S. Atomic Energy Commission's Nevada Test Site and Nuclear Rocket Development Station*. Los Alamos, New Mexico: LA-4125, Los Alamos Scientific Laboratory, 1969

III. Interviews

William McKinnis, October 21, 2002

About the Author

Recalling the Past!
(**NTS badge photo**)

I was born in Batavia, New York, but grew up in nearby Niagara Falls. After obtaining a Mechanical Engineering degree from Rensselaer Polytechnic Institute, Troy, New York, I served as a Lieutenant in the Army Ordinance Corps at Aberdeen Proving Grounds, Maryland. In 1959, I joined the (then) Lawrence Radiation Laboratory at the Nevada Test Site to work on a nuclear ramjet reactor program in Jackass Flat. It was there I first brushed against history on the Test Site as a visitor to the ghost town of Wahmonie and the Hornsilver Mine. Living in the government dormitories in the town of Mercury, I spent weekends with friends exploring many of the historical areas

of the Test Site that are chronicled in *Before the Nukes*. In 1967, I moved to Livermore, California to continue my career at Lawrence Livermore National Laboratory, retiring in 1996. Shortly before retiring, I published my first book, *Autorental Europe - A Guide to Choosing and Driving a Car in Europe. Before the Nukes* was born out of research done for *Able Site*, a mystery novel set on the Test Site. It is currently a work in progress.